THE PEOPLE'S CONSTITUTION

by

Nathaniel Downes

Printed on demand.

First Edition, 2016

ISBN 978-1537783567

The People's Constitution

The Constitution began with these bold words, a brave statement to set forth the course of a nation.

> *We the People of the United States, in Order to form a more perfect Union, establish Justice, insure domestic Tranquility, provide for the common defence, promote the general Welfare, and secure the Blessings of Liberty to ourselves and our Posterity, do ordain and establish this Constitution for the United States of America.*

For the latter 18th century, this statement was unheard of, a revolution against the establishment. A government not set by a monarch's decree, or by an imperial edict, but one set up by the people themselves in order to form a union reflecting their values. This revolutionary act changed the course of history, and has been under attack by revisionists who would seek to recreate the very oligarchy which the nation had thrown off.

Since 1789, the United States has functioned under this document, this framework drafted at the Constitutional Convention held in Philadelphia. Replacing the dysfunctional Articles of Confederation, the United States Constitution has held strong despite enemies from both within and without.

Now it faces its gravest challenge ever. A cult of selfishness has taken root and perverted the rhetoric discussing the Constitution in order to push their agenda of greed and avarice. These would-be Oligarchs, for there is no better name for them, are found both within the wealthiest of our nation as well as those who strive to join them. Together, they have made it their agenda to grossly abuse the people of the United States, and their goal to secure absolute power for themselves.

They began subtly, by creating an alternate interpretation of the Constitution. They knew, like the founding fathers did, that the US Constitution was a living document, not a dead piece of parchment. It was written such that it could, and should, be interpreted not on the ideals of the late 18th century Enlightenment, but on the era in which the citizens of the United States currently lived. This is how and why the United States has held strong over the centuries – it could adapt as the times changed.

By introducing their alternative interpretation, one structured to benefit only them, the goal was to over time change the way in which the United States functioned. Over a century of work it took, with some setbacks, but now it has stuck, and their policies, ones designed to give them absolute power at the expensive of the people the Constitution was drafted to protect, have taken over.

Their model of the Constitution was one in which corporations were people, that their CEO's religious views trumped yours, where money is speech, and where the people have no say in the running of their own government. This is the model whose endgame is nothing less than the end of the great experiment which is the United States of America and the creation of a new, class-driven society much like we found in the middle ages.

With this model in place, corporations with more money can drown out the speech of the people, influencing politics for their own agendas by outspending the voters and advocates, or by locking them out of the public dialog through purchase in media outlets. They seek to have the people pay for their mistakes, while they keep the rewards for their successes – and they have framed their interpretation of the Constitution to accomplish this.

Arguing for a nonsensical idea, "Originalism," the argument goes that the US Constitution is to only be interpreted one way, and one way only — that of the oligarch's fantasy founding fathers. The originalists proclaim a fiction that the founding fathers "original intent" of the Constitution as defense of the oligarch's ideas and wishes. This viewpoint presents the founding fathers as near divine beings holding a single unified vision for the future.

To prevent disruption, they have paid for scholars, researchers and historians to back their claims. They cite each other, as if an incestuous family tree – each branch feeding information to the others with the intent to disguise the lies. Honest historians checking on this claim of intent have always fallen short of validating the claims, but the truth is dwarfed by the cascading noise of lies from the oligarch propaganda machine.

The wealthy learned this trick from another group, those who would seek to empower and enrich themselves using the word of whichever deity they proclaim to do so. While religious charlatans have existed since the time we first harnessed fire, this new wave sought to establish a new religious theocracy within the United States through reinterpreting our governments framework. In so doing, this then becomes the most extreme form of reinterpretation of the Constitution, requiring the actual abandonment of the language it holds to create a new framework with which to enslave their followers.

They accomplished this through having the document, the framework, subject to their own holy review, not available for the people direct. Handed out as holy scripture rather than a legal framework, the Constitution then becomes a weapon for these holy terrors to use against the people, to suppress them and enabling the oligarchs to seize absolute power without fear. This should come as no surprise once it is understood that they do the same thing for their own holy books.

This unholy alliance invents out of whole cloth language and cherry pick elements to create their narrative. They make fanciful claims, create noise to disguise the origin of those claims and pray nobody ever checks on them. The monetary oligarchs seek to extract as much money out of the people as possible, and these religious oligarchs seek

6

to create a religious state in the same vein as the Taliban—one guided by a strict religious interpretation. In both cases, these interpretations are ones which they created, and now are in many ways dominating the discussion on our Constitution.

This is the problem those of us who know and love this country face. Setting aside labels a moment, there is a love people have for their nation. It is only natural. The United States is an unusual design however in that it is not one nation, but a federation of nations in a united structure – 50 nations forged into one. This creates a sense of pride, of uniqueness in the world which can be tapped by those to move this nation forward; or exploited by those who would seek to pervert it to their private, selfish ends.

Our nation was not founded on the principle of competition, but on cooperation, of working together for the greater good. Yet it is competition which our current political system, developed through narrow interpretations drafted by these Oligarchs, forces upon us.

Those who would subvert our Constitution hope that this nature, the inherent idea of a living document, is forgotten. This is why we find arguments for strict interpretations so long as it benefits them, and why lessons on our own history are forgotten. After all, we only need to turn to our countries own founding fathers to find letters such as this from Thomas Jefferson to Samuel Kercheval:

> Some men look at constitutions with sanctimonious reverence, and deem them like the arc of the covenant, too sacred to be touched. They ascribe to the men of the preceding age a wisdom more than human, and suppose what they did to be beyond amendment. I knew that age well; I belonged to it, and labored with it. It deserved well of its country. It was very like the present, but without the experience of the present; and forty years of experience in government is worth a century of book-reading; and this they would say themselves, were they to rise from the dead. I am certainly not an advocate for frequent and untried changes in laws and constitutions. I think moderate imperfections had better be borne with; because, when once known, we accommodate ourselves to them, and find practical means of correcting their ill effects. But I know also, that laws and institutions must go hand in hand with the progress of the human mind. As that becomes more developed, more enlightened, as new discoveries are made, new truths disclosed, and manners and opinions change with the change of circumstances, institutions must advance also, and keep pace with the times. We might as well require a man to wear still the coat which fitted him when a boy, as civilized society to remain ever under the regimen of their barbarous ancestors

He was not alone in his view that the Constitution was not a holy document, to only be interpreted and understood with religious zealotry. Our founders saw the Constitution as a living document to be read and understood by everyone, and in the era in which the readers live. To do otherwise is to render the government created by that framework not only doomed to obsolescence, but actually harmful. The Articles of Confederation was a problem clear in their mind, and it was not even a decade old before its rigidity became a hindrance and it had to be replaced.

As such, the founding fathers admitted that they did not share a unified vision at all. Daniel Webster wished for far different than Alexander Hamilton, and as such both did view James Madison's ideas with skepticism. Their ideas were as diverse as they themselves were. Finding out some "original intent" from an eclectic collection of farmers, businessmen, tradesmen and politicians who barely shared a common language would be no more accurate than discerning their intent from reading tea leaves.

Instead, our founders understood that it was compromise, the reaching of a mutual agreement, which was critical for our nation. And once a compromise was reached, it was critical for all to adhere to the drafted solution. Rigid interpretations and ideological purity were the enemy of the republic, not virtues to adhere to. Without the coming together of different viewpoints, and discipline to unify around a compromise solution, our nation would have collapsed centuries ago, as it nearly did under the rigid predecessor of the US Constitution, the Articles of Confederation. They had witnessed this first hand, and designed their framework going forward accordingly.

If we wish to save the United States, we must take back the Constitution from those who would pervert it for their own selfish ends, who would destroy it from within. To do that, the first step is to reject their interpretation of the Constitution, and to first rediscover the words which our founding fathers put quill down to parchment all those years ago. Then, it must be interpreted by the era in which we live, the 21st century, not the 18th.

To understand the Constitution, to understand the nature of it, and how it can apply in modern society, we need to look back on these words with a realization that when written, humans were sailing in wind powered ships, the very idea of a railroad was preposterous. If you were to tell them that in under 200 years a man would step onto the moon wearing the flag of the United States on his sleeve, you were most likely to be mocked or ridiculed for even entertaining such a notion. How can a governmental framework drafted in such a time even function today?

It is only through contemporary interpretation, and understanding the time in which we now live in, which would enable its function. By reading it with new eyes, and not trying to force your vision to match an artificial fantasy of an era in which Napoleon walked the battlefield of Europe, one can begin to move forward and free ourselves of this death spiral which we find ourselves in.

This solution is little different than the methods used by the would-be oligarchs. The difference is that while they aim to interpret it for their own selfish ends, we can interpret it for the benefit of all. We the People deserve nothing less than to take back our nation, and to reclaim the Constitution which was written for us from those who seek to use it for selfish ends.

After all, that is what this nation was founded on in the first place.

Article. I.

Section. 1.

All legislative Powers herein granted shall be vested in a Congress of the United States, which shall consist of a Senate and House of Representatives.

Most nations use a legislative body of some form. In the United Kingdom, they have a Parliament, in Cuba you find the National Assembly, but whatever the name, this representative body is common among nations of all ilk. The US Constitution is interesting here in that it vests only legislative power in our representative body, our Congress. Many other nations, including the aforementioned United Kingdom and Cuba, have their congress handling both legislative, the writing of the laws, and executive, the execution of the laws.

Someone must write the laws, and historically, a legislative body has been one of the more equitable methods to do so. In the US Constitution, the legislative body is to be split into two parts, a Senate and a House of Representatives. At this point, there is not much which needs to be interpreted, as it is very straightforward.

But the division itself gives us an indication both as to the power granted in this agency, but in how it operates. Each half of this legislature is to have its own methods, its own processes, but need to work in partnership with the other.

By being divided, it prevents single body dominance over the state. This shows us how powerful, and important, the legislature is.

Section. 2.

The House of Representatives shall be composed of Members chosen every second Year by the People of the several States, and the Electors in each State shall have the Qualifications requisite for Electors of the most numerous Branch of the State Legislature.

In setting up the House of Representatives, our founders set forth a system whereby the House shall reflect upon the various state legislatures. Those who actually elect these members are called here Electors. The qualification for Electors is set forth as the same as for the most numerous branch of the State Legislature. This put much of the power for this house in each states hands.

However, by doing so it also reduced power as well. For, one state may have one set of requirements, while a different state may use yet another. This meant that the House was internally, and purposefully, inconsistent with its electoral process. It is not hard to figure that the authors presumed each state would develop their own unique methods for handling their state legislatures, and therefore would each have their own requirements for Electors.

Now here is where interpretation begins, where we were envisioning it one way, but which can be handled differently. House members are chosen by Electors, which have to meet the same qualifications as those who elect the state legislatures. Interpretation then comes not from any change to the House members themselves, but to the state legislatures. Members who are elected by these Electors are in turn classified as Representatives.

In the traditional interpretation, the state governments elected their Members through direct popular election in districts. The locking each seat within the House to an individual district, the result of a series of bills passed by congress, the latest one in 1967 and residing at 2 U.S. Code § 2c, is one of the methods used to freeze out minority voices in this nation, to eliminate popular movements which do not meet the current political climate. There is no reason why this interpretation must be adhered to, however.

Let us adjust a moment, and consider other approaches for Electors.

It could be argued that having unique districts for House Members could be unconstitutional. After all, it states that the qualifications are based on that of the state legislatures. It can be said that the qualifications extend to the state legislature districts themselves. If this interpretation was to be adhered to, this would then require that federal districts be based upon state districts, directly.

In many nations there are be both direct district elections as well as allocated by party preference. Political parties are a reality in modern society, so rather than having them an adjunct to the process, able to manipulate the process itself due to their divorced state, these nations integrate them into the process itself. If done on the state level in such a way which makes manipulation far more difficult and far less rewarding for the parties themselves, it could be carried forward and applied nationally. Elections then become allocated by party preference, rather than a winner-takes-all methodology, and would be allocated by party elites who oversee the system.

Another avenue would be to use a direct, proportional system for representative election. Rather than a single district holding a single seat, they would hold 3 or more. However, a vote would remain for a single candidate, and the election would be split proportionately using a method such as Single Transferable Vote. By so doing, a more direct representation with the voter could be accomplished.

Lastly, there is also the option of taking this power away from the common people entirely, for a more meritocratic method. At no point does the Constitution claim that Electors are the same as the People, or even voters. An indirect election method, where local bodies themselves elect higher governmental bodies, would be fully lawful under the US Constitution, so long as it was uniform from within the state from which the federal legislators came from.

The US Constitution made the exact nature of our legislature, indeed, our government itself, something of a mystery to be solved over time by the people currently living within it. And each state then is free to develop the system which works best for the

People within.

> *No Person shall be a Representative who shall not have attained to the Age of twenty five Years, and been seven Years a Citizen of the United States, and who shall not, when elected, be an Inhabitant of that State in which he shall be chosen.*

This is a fairly straightforward section, with little interpretation needed. To serve in the House of Representatives, either as a Member or Elector, you must be 25, have been a citizen of the US for seven years, and must reside within the state you are to Represent.

This points back however to the earlier discussion. It does not specify living in the district, but the state itself. This implies that the idea of a congressman was not to represent a small district, but to represent the state as a whole. Indeed, if we review the first congresses, we find that statewide, also known as at-large, congressional seats were quite common.

This is how our system was envisioned to work, but over the centuries we have forgotten this principle, neglected the demands of our society. And this is not something out of our power, out of our reach, to resolve.

By reducing the number of districts, so most states would have only one, we eliminate a lot of the problems we find in our federal government. Through consolidation of territory, while maintaining the seats in general available, we further erode the power to manipulate the electorate, for candidates to pick their voters, and help establish honest representation.

> *Representatives and direct Taxes shall be apportioned among the several States which may be included within this Union, according to their respective Numbers, which shall be determined by adding to the whole Number of free Persons, including those bound to Service for a Term of Years, and excluding Indians not taxed, three fifths of all other Persons. The actual Enumeration shall be made within three Years after the first Meeting of the Congress of the United States, and within every subsequent Term of ten Years, in such Manner as they shall by Law direct. The Number of Representatives shall not exceed one for every thirty Thousand, but each State shall have at Least one Representative; and until such enumeration shall be made, the State of New Hampshire shall be entitled to chuse three, Massachusetts eight, Rhode-Island and Providence Plantations one, Connecticut five, New-York six, New Jersey four, Pennsylvania eight, Delaware one, Maryland six, Virginia ten, North Carolina five, South Carolina five, and Georgia three.*

Much of this is historical, and portions have been amended by the 14th Amendment which we will analyze later on. But, what remains is that congress has the power to apportion taxes based on population, and specifying that representation, and taxation, is to be determined primarily by the number of free persons, excluding native populations entirely, and only 3/5ths of non-free people. At the time, the interpretation was that non-free people was to include slaves, but with the repeal of slavery within the United States, properly this portion is no longer in effect.

However, there are many in this country who we cannot honestly consider free. The United States has the largest prison population in the world. Are those we lock up for petty crimes free? No, by our own laws and traditions, they are not free persons, therefore they should still fall under this provision of the US Constitution, save they too are addressed by the 14th amendment in part, covering those currently serving a sentence. Yet, we have millions of people who have served their sentences, who have not had their voting rights restored. Can these people be called free? Let us consider them not free.

This may seem odd, but consider the changes to policy nationwide which this would bring. What would happen is that states which enact strict criminal law would be penalizing themselves by taking away representation. With this interpretation, Texas, which has stripped the voting rights of one out of every 22 citizens at its peak due to being a former convict, would have lost a Representative. That becomes a severe penalty as over-prosecution and draconian punishments that extend past the convict's sentence are imposed. California facing similar penalties would have the potential to lose two congressional seats with this adjustment.

With an adjustment of interpretation here, we create a disincentive for the prison-industrial complex which is growing in this nation. Severe criminal penalties, instead of rehabilitation and treatment, now carry with them a punitive measure for those states which enact them. Now, a measure which in the past was interpreted as being for slavery becomes a section which stands against the rise of the prison-state, a clearly winning proposition. After all, none in our nation want to see the growth of prison camps, which is the inevitable end of the oligarchs movement to criminalize behavior.

And when we get to the 14th Amendment, which does edit this section, this change becomes crucial for the prevention of the police state.

> *When vacancies happen in the Representation from any State, the Executive Authority thereof shall issue Writs of Election to fill such Vacancies.*

When a vacancy happens, it is up to the executive authority of the state from whence the vacancy occurred to fill them using whatever methods the state deems appropriate. In every state so far admitted to the union, this is a governor, but is not exclusively limited to such a title. This has little room for direct interpretation, but instead is a reminder of how important state governments are, and how they need to be included in any movement forward away from the Oligarchy.

However, that they did not specify the governor, but the Executive Authority, means that in turn, we are not limited by a mere governor. This frees up states for development of alternative methods to handle executive authority than the mere replication of existing systems. Perhaps a First Minister, or an Executive Council would be in place. By being open ended, it leaves us open as well to the possibilities for avenues which would help to empower the people themselves.

> *The House of Representatives shall chuse their Speaker and other Officers; and shall have the sole Power of Impeachment.*

It is clear that the House of Representatives was to have presiding officers, including a Speaker, upon reading the Constitution. In addition, they were the sole entity charged with the power of impeachment.

Now, the role of the speaker is one which predates the US Constitution, which is why it is maintained here. Its origins can be found in the Parliament of the United Kingdom, where the House of Commons elects a speaker to act as its presiding officer. The speaker has a very specific duty, to oversee order within the house. They preside over debates, determining who can speak, for how long, and has the right to mete out minor punishments to members of the house who violate the chamber rules.

By rights, the Speaker role must be non-partisan, and under the British system they renounce any and all political affiliations for the term of their role as speaker. This is how the role of speaker was understood by the framers of the US Constitution, and is the interpretation we will hold here. By making it a non-partisan role, rather than the current setup of the speaker being also a political parties majority leader, it changes the dynamic of the way in which the House conducts business. In addition, this vote for is to appoint officers, which again in the British methodology included such things as deputies, chairmen of various committees, and the sergeant-at-arms. By being tied to the selection of the speaker, these deputies and chairmen too, it must be said, be non-partisan positions.

By taking a more founder-centric understanding of this interpretation, we can begin to erode the partisan gridlock which often times causes disruption in our political process. Right now, many of the offices which need to be above partisan politics are embroiled in them, compromising the integrity of their position. This in turn makes the political parties themselves less effective, as they now have an incentive to function as a power broker rather than as a caucusing and campaigning agency. This in turn erodes their leaderships ability to actually arrange elections, as they must spend more time balancing the parliamentary process which congress itself needs to function.

It must be noted that the role of the Speaker is not limited to a sitting member of the House of Representatives, nor the role of the various officers. This will be addressed in further detail later on, as another provision puts a further restriction on all officers. With these officers as non-partisan positions, it would be in Congresses best interest to use outside members to fill this role. The men who wrote the Constitution were of this belief and in a latter section of the Constitution would all but demand it. Perhaps former Representatives who had left office. Perhaps influential judges would fill this role. Perhaps even former Presidents would enjoy the opportunity to keep congress in line. Whomever is chosen, however, would be there to do their job for the people, not for the party.

In addition, the House has been given the Power of Impeachment. Contrary to popular viewpoint, impeachment does not mean removal of office. Impeachment is the process by which an elected official is charged with a crime. This means that any suspected criminal activity against an elected official on the federal level is to be formally charged only by the House of Representatives.

This is the sole function of the House in impeachment proceedings, the levying of a charge upon an elected official. Anything further must go to the Senate.

Section. 3.

The Senate of the United States shall be composed of two Senators from each State, chosen by the Legislature thereof, for six Years; and each Senator shall have one Vote.

We have adjusted how Senators are appointed since the Constitution was written with the 17th Amendment. Originally, the Senators were chosen by the state legislatures directly. As such, the Senators were expected to represent the state governments themselves, and not the people of the states.

Even with the changes brought about by the 17th Amendment, we have not changed the nature of the Senate. Each Senator will serve for six years, and each state has two of them. What is noticed however is that there is no clear definition if the Senators are to be chosen at once, or are independent in term from one another. At this time, we have decided that Senators are elected independently, each one serving their own term in the Senate. This is not the only possible avenue to interpret however.

The goal within the Constitution was to give states more direct influence over national policy preventing mob rule which population based representation may lead to. But it still was to represent the People of the state, and what they stood for.

To help engineer what was desired, let us change how we elect these members a moment, and have both Senators chosen at the same time. But, let us use a proportional method, complete with single transferable voting. The People would vote for one senator, and the allotment would be proportionally allocated based on the turnout. This would vary the mechanism of power within the Senate, and for the states themselves, while also making the Senate not only more representative, but also better able to serve in its role.

This would also highlight the power within the states themselves, and in turn improve the role of the Senate in American politics.

Immediately after they shall be assembled in Consequence of the first Election, they shall be divided as equally as may be into three Classes. The Seats of the Senators of the first Class shall be vacated at the Expiration of the second Year, of the second Class at the Expiration of the fourth Year, and of the third Class at the Expiration of the sixth Year, so that one third may be chosen every second Year; and if Vacancies happen by Resignation, or otherwise, during the Recess of the Legislature of any State, the Executive thereof may make temporary Appointments until the next Meeting of the Legislature, which shall then fill such Vacancies.

The vacancy requirement was also changed by the 17th Amendment, which we will be dealing with in a later chapter. But, for the remaining portion, it created a rolling membership, where a third of all Senators would have their terms expire every federal election cycle, every two years.

This made the Senate more stable, and consistent than the House of Representatives. By having 6-year terms, a Senator could plan for the longer term. However, with a third being replaced every two years, it also means that consistency is per-seat, with the makeup of the Senate shifting with the elections just as with the House.

By shifting elections to per-state instead of per-seat, this rolling membership would not shift by much at all. It would however make each state's Senate pair more akin to a partnership than isolated seats.

> No Person shall be a Senator who shall not have attained to the Age of thirty Years, and been nine Years a Citizen of the United States, and who shall not, when elected, be an Inhabitant of that State for which he shall be chosen.

Much like the similar passage for the House of Representatives, there are qualifications to be Senator. You must be 30 years old, having been a citizen of the United States for no less than 9, and must reside within the state which they are to represent in the Senate.

> The Vice President of the United States shall be President of the Senate, but shall have no Vote, unless they be equally divided.

The process for electing the Vice President is addressed in Article 2. What we find here is one area of difference between the Senate and the House, and how it is to function. While the Speaker of the House is to be a non-partisan position, the President of the Senate is instead a partisan position – indeed he is selected by the same electors as the president under our current system. Like the Speaker, the President of the Senate oversees parliamentary process. Unlike the Speaker, the President of the Senate is expected to vote in times of division. No such provision to enable the speaker to vote can be found for the House.

We will explore the Vice President's role in greater detail under this interpretation when we come to the executive section of the US Constitution.

> The Senate shall chuse their other Officers, and also a President pro tempore, in the Absence of the Vice President, or when he shall exercise the Office of President of the United States.

At this point we see a similar officers selection to the House, but with a special officer to fill in for the Vice President when absent or when exercising the office of President. Since it has already been established earlier that unlike the House, under this interpretation of the Constitution the Senate is more likely to be governed by party politics and less by caucuses and parliamentary process, it is only logical for these officers to be partisan positions. This only makes sense with the election process as discussed earlier – being in office for three election cycles compared to one enables them to take a longer view. With Senators selected as one and of the same group, statewide, they could then serve as the state's mechanism for creating a vision of the future.

> The Senate shall have the sole Power to try all Impeachments. When sitting for that Purpose, they shall be on Oath or Affirmation. When the President of the United States is tried, the Chief Justice shall

preside: And no Person shall be convicted without the Concurrence of two thirds of the Members present.

Once the house has charged an elected official, a process called Impeachment, the Senate then has the power to put the official on trial. A conviction requires a super-majority of 2/3rds of Senators. When the President is on trial, the Chief Justice shall preside over the proceedings, in place of the Vice President who would, it presumes, replace a sitting President should they be removed from office.

Why this arrangement is done is so as to prevent any one house of congress from seizing full control over the Government. If the legislature finds it needed to remove a sitting President, it must have the highest seat from the Supreme Court overseeing the process. That means two branches are needed to remove an issue within the third. A balancing act indeed.

Judgment in Cases of Impeachment shall not extend further than to removal from Office, and disqualification to hold and enjoy any Office of honor, Trust or Profit under the United States: but the Party convicted shall nevertheless be liable and subject to Indictment, Trial, Judgment and Punishment, according to Law.

The most severe penalty which can be levied against an elected official is removal of office, the disqualification from ever holding future office, and the elimination of any and all benefits thereof. However, an impeachment conviction does not prevent further prosecution under a civil or criminal court either. The key is to recall that an impeachment is not a conviction of wrongdoing, but the charging, and a trial in the Senate must take place to convict.

And a conviction does not necessitate the removal from office either. They limited the most severe penalties, but not the least. Once you combine the powers as given elsewhere in the Constitution, should a legislature find that the President is not executing his duties for a particular law, say not enforcing an anti-trust act, they could impeach, convict, and then have another officer execute that duty in the President's stead as punishment. The President would have his authority to act on that subject eliminated as a result, a censure with far more teeth than the way we currently envision.

Over the centuries, the role and nature of impeachment has been lost. It needs to be restored, and a reminder to all People, that it is not some special or unique construct, but a formal process for something which happens regularly in this nation only applied to elected officials.

Section. 4.

The Times, Places and Manner of holding Elections for Senators and Representatives, shall be prescribed in each State by the Legislature thereof; but the Congress may at any time by Law make or alter such Regulations, except as to the Places of chusing Senators.

Here we have the states managing elections. Part of the checks and balances of the system we can find here, and also why we can discuss the idea of following this interpretation of the US Constitution, which would give better representation to the People. By knowing of how the system is supposed to work, we can then work together to make it happen.

It will require focusing efforts on the states themselves. This is not even a difficult task, due to the way state politics works. It does require being aware of the end goal, and of holding the course. The Oligarchs have been working for centuries, and we cannot undo their damage overnight.

> *The Congress shall assemble at least once in every Year, and such Meeting shall be on the first Monday in December, unless they shall by Law appoint a different Day.*

This portion has been modified by the 20th Amendment, which will be discussed later. But the remaining portion is that Congress is to assemble at least once a year. This prevents the nation from having an absentee government. It also is notable that congress is given the same day, regardless of which house we are discussing. When combined with latter provisions, it is clear that both houses were to legislate together, as well as independently as they now operate.

Consider how a joint legislative system would work for a moment. This would, I'd imagine, be for important bills, such as spending measures. House members and Senators would each have their own roles to play in the process. For one, the Speaker of the House would retain the ability to call bills for a vote, a role defined above. Senators would be there for planning and strategic vision. House members would be for hammering out the details once the longer term visions have been set.

By forcing the two houses to work cooperatively for a measure, it would also serve to break down the issues we often find between these two bodies of our legislature. All too often, bills, important bills, pass from one side to the other, and languish, forgotten. Even a single session per year forcing them to cooperate for a day would do wonders for resolving this sometimes vast chasm within which bills fall to their doom.

Section. 5.

> *Each House shall be the Judge of the Elections, Returns and Qualifications of its own Members, and a Majority of each shall constitute a Quorum to do Business; but a smaller Number may adjourn from day to day, and may be authorized to compel the Attendance of absent Members, in such Manner, and under such Penalties as each House may provide.*

This measure allows each house of Congress to evaluate the elections in the states which elect members of Congress. This is to give a uniform standard for Representatives. So, if someone shows up claiming to have been elected, but without the same level of documentation as every other member, they would be turned away.

The need for a Quorum is well known, it prevents a minority from forcing through legislation without due process. At least 50% +1 members need to be in attendance before any legislature can be voted on. Smaller numbers can gather for hearings, or smaller debates, but without a quorum, no legislation can pass in either house of Congress.

Also, either house can, if the rules permit, compel members to appear. This is to prevent a group from holding legislation hostage by preventing enough members of congress to gather for a quorum.

To ensure a Quorum, the Constitution tasks Congress with assigning people to maintain attendance. This smaller group is given the power to levy penalties in accordance with the rules that Congress sets. There is no provision however that this smaller group be limited to either house. It could even be theorized that a single group made up of members from each house is tasked with this duty.

This is actually the provision which required the Civil War. When the southern states attempted to leave the union, they took enough numbers that calling a quorum was not as easy a practical matter. While there remained enough seats to call a quorum, there was still argument that a compelling of attendance was required. As a result, by acting as they did, rather than to leave the union, the secessionists only made the civil war effectively required, under the US Constitution.

Each House may determine the Rules of its Proceedings, punish its Members for disorderly Behaviour, and, with the Concurrence of two thirds, expel a Member.

The rules for each house are decided by the members of that house. It is a form of gentleman's agreement for how to behave. It also allows for congress to self-police, and punish those who violate these rules, and even with a super-majority to expel a troublesome member of congress.

These rules are not set in stone, and can be determined at the start of each congress. They do not change often, but they can and do change.

This is also what happened during the civil war for those members of congress who left to join the confederacy. They were removed from their positions, and the state governments charged with finding replacements. During the civil war, most of the southern states had representation on the federal level, who continued to operate as part of the United States during this period. By attempting to secede, the confederates actually eroded their support and their voice on the federal level. Rather than demonstrating power, they threw it away.

Truly, an irony which was lost on the rebels.

Each House shall keep a Journal of its Proceedings, and from time to time publish the same, excepting such Parts as may in their Judgment require Secrecy; and the Yeas and Nays of the Members of either House on any question shall, at the Desire of one fifth of those Present, be entered on the Journal.

Record keeping is important in every democracy. Over the years, both houses of Congress have used various tricks to opt out of recording the individual votes, through the use of verbal acclamation for example on measures where the actual voting record could be controversial. Their interpretation is that by merely recording that a verbal passage was done, this section is met. Their interpretation is that the desire to record is independent of the passage of the measure itself.

The proposal here is to be far stricter in the interpretation – that as written, this clearly demands that votes, precisely who votes yay or nay, to always be recorded and part of record. That if the affirmative vote for a measure is of at least a fifth of those present, it must be recorded in the journal, as part of the actual voting process. This would prevent measures that have no support from being recorded while preventing votes that could be called into question from being masqueraded.

This ability to disguise positions, to hide ones record, is against the principle of this passage. A stricter interpretation of it is needed in order to help overcome the distrust in our government which has taken grip. By having these details public knowledge, and widely disseminated, can the People best govern themselves. Secrets enable the continuation of lies, of deception, and of distortions, the three true enemies of democracy.

> *Neither House, during the Session of Congress, shall, without the Consent of the other, adjourn for more than three days, nor to any other Place than that in which the two Houses shall be sitting.*

Congress must meet at the same general time, not independently. This requires both houses to cooperate in balancing legislation. It also requires that congress holds its sessions in the actual congressional building, to prevent one from effectively going rogue and hold a show get-together in some fancy resort in order to vacation on the taxpayers dime without any work being done.

There is already some issue of one or more houses doing tricks to prevent actually meeting. Having one person show up, hit the gavel to open the session, and hitting it again a minute later to close it being a prime example of it. This would therefore lack a quorum, so would not qualify as in-session under our interpretation here.

By doing so, the legislature is failing to engage in their lawful and elected duties. They are engaging in time-wasting activities, rather than addressing the tasks for which they were elected to high office to begin with. The system as implemented is clearly not how intended, and it must be brought to heel.

And, if we took this passage, with the earlier ones on face value, these actions of single member opening of session could not be done and meet the constitutional requirement if interpreted our way. Failure to bring a quorum for the session would render said sessions null and void.

This is the correct and needed interpretation for modern times. Since earlier there was a demand for a quorum in order to claim a session is being held, all that is required is this standard – for a session to be held, people must actually show up.

By doing this it limits parliamentary tricks which are used to block legislation, or to prevent action, so prevalent in modern politics. By interpreting this in a strict quorum manner, it holds congress more accountable, and forces them to actually address the issues at-hand rather than dancing around them.

In addition, by being strict on the attendance and location requirements we can prevent other tricks common in today's legislature. There have been multiple votes where members of congress have been hidden away in another room, or even held in another building, to prevent them from casting a vote. If interpreted in this way, this tactic can backfire on whomever attempts to do it, as will be explained later on.

Section. 6.

The Senators and Representatives shall receive a Compensation for their Services, to be ascertained by Law, and paid out of the Treasury of the United States. They shall in all Cases, except Treason, Felony and Breach of the Peace, be privileged from Arrest during their Attendance at the Session of their respective Houses, and in going to and returning from the same; and for any Speech or Debate in either House, they shall not be questioned in any other Place.

This section covers multiple areas as you can see. In the current interpretation, Members of Congress are to be paid for their service. With this interpretation, they also cannot be arrested. It has been modified by the 27th Amendment as well, which we will be discussing later on.

This interpretation is a very simplistic view, and does not properly address what is listed here. The sections which are considered immune from arrest are not anywhere near as broad as claimed. Read it over again. The privilege of being exempted from arrest is tied to their attendance to the congressional session, and to the travel to and from it. It does not give them generalized immunity from arrest as written. It can be argued that a Member of Congress can be arrested, convicted, and serve time in jail, so long as they can still manage to attend to their duties.

They cannot be arrested as part of a political game however. Any attempt to arrest them would effectively result in their automatic attendance to the session. The attempt to use the power of congressional arrest would instead grant the accused the podium upon which to deal with the attempt to stifle political opposition.

The second portion is even more interesting, they are being privileged from being questioned on any speech or debate in relation to criminal cases. This is usually just folded in with the first to give a sweeping immunity from legal issues. But, this is very specific as well, it covers only speech or debate within either House. It is here to prevent the persecution of political enemies.

But it is not adhered to very well, as even a casual examination of the "Red Scare" of the 1950's will tell you. More than one member of congress had their positions questioned in this manner, including the powerful Senator Millard Tydings of Maryland – and those who would be your new Oligarchs want it that way. Obey them, or else have your ability to do your job and help run the government compromised through legal entanglements.

Changing this interpretation would prevent such tactics from taking root. This is a country founded on the bringing together of different ideas. By rejecting one, by labeling any who hold it as an enemy, this is a rejection of the nature of the US

Constitution itself. We will never agree to everything, but it is when we change a disagreement into a reason to shut down the debate, we have failed as a nation.

Yes, this means that ideas we do not agree with will be held, and shared. Not everyone will agree with our ideas as well. A strict interpretation of this, that all viewpoints may be shared freely and not punished for having, is obviously needed in order to accomplish lasting reform in our government.

It can be further expanded that the calling into question could even put the nature of our political campaigns into question. After all, what else are negative campaigns but the calling into question of that given in speech or debate in the court of public opinion.

Changing our interpretation here, it would make the current negative campaign environment nearly impossible. It would instead force incumbents to run on their actual voting record, and prevent the introduction of most forms of negative campaign advertising. This of course does not prohibit fact checking, which is verification and not questioning. Nor does it prohibit attacks on character. But it does prevent the form of open ended questions which lie at the heart of many negative campaigns run in this country.

> No Senator or Representative shall, during the Time for which he was elected, be appointed to any civil Office under the Authority of the United States, which shall have been created, or the Emoluments whereof shall have been encreased during such time; and no Person holding any Office under the United States, shall be a Member of either House during his Continuance in Office.

This section's goal is to prevent any member of congress from holding another office within the federal government. By doing so, it prevented the consolidation of power into too few of hands. A president who was also a congressman, or supreme court justice, or all three, would have undue influence over politics. This section as interpreted today however is being limited to only applying to certain offices and not others, which is not as it is written here.

Recall, earlier in the Constitution, both houses of congress were to elect people to office, such as the Speaker of the House and the President Pro-Tempore. If we interpret that our Constitution was to prevent these positions from becoming partisan, and that both of these sections apply to the same officers, this causes a conflict with these two sections if those office holders are part of either house.

The easiest solution is what was mentioned earlier, not to have them as Members of Congress. By divorcing these officers from the houses which they are to support, we erode the power currently wielded in each while also adding a layer of accountability sorely lacking in modern politics. Right now, we have severe issues of congressional officers playing politics with procedure, of freezing out legislature or legislators in order to punish them politically. This is not how our government was designed to work, and it needs to stop.

By interpreting this section strictly, that the very officers who are to manage out congress cannot themselves be members of congress, we divorce them from the petty trickery which has permeated our federal system. It then also enables for a more continuing form of governance, these officers would no longer be directly affected by party politics so would continue from congress to congress.

Their jobs, as defined by the constitution, would be to oversee the body politic, not be part of the body politic.

Section. 7.

All Bills for raising Revenue shall originate in the House of Representatives; but the Senate may propose or concur with Amendments as on other Bills.

This puts the power of the purse, the power of taxation, square on the shoulders of the House of Representatives. The purpose of this is to ensure that the People had their voices heard on taxation. Recall, the Revolutionary War began with a single phrase, "No Taxation Without Representation." Our current system does not represent us well, but in revisiting the earlier sections and interpreting them to meet the demands of a modern society should go a long way to resolving this.

These changes also alter this section in a not subtle manner. By having a more representative body, the house now has a stronger argument for the power of taxation than it does today. There are ways by which the Senate can propose bills which can and do raise revenue, typically through the use of parliamentary procedure such as stripping another bill of all or nearly all text and adding the new bill as an amendment. Overall however, the house controls all revenue. This will become very important to pay attention to later on.

Every Bill which shall have passed the House of Representatives and the Senate, shall, before it become a Law, be presented to the President of the United States; If he approve he shall sign it, but if not he shall return it, with his Objections to that House in which it shall have originated, who shall enter the Objections at large on their Journal, and proceed to reconsider it. If after such Reconsideration two thirds of that House shall agree to pass the Bill, it shall be sent, together with the Objections, to the other House, by which it shall likewise be reconsidered, and if approved by two thirds of that House, it shall become a Law. But in all such Cases the Votes of both Houses shall be determined by yeas and Nays, and the Names of the Persons voting for and against the Bill shall be entered on the Journal of each House respectively. If any Bill shall not be returned by the President within ten Days (Sundays excepted) after it shall have been presented to him, the Same shall be a Law, in like Manner as if he had signed it, unless the Congress by their Adjournment prevent its Return, in which Case it shall not be a Law.

Now here is a section where the current interpretation allows for a lot of abuse. As it sits, the interpretation is that the president is given the power to veto a bill, to reject it completely out of hand. Congress has the authority to overcome that veto using a 2/3rd super-majority in both houses. It also gives a time limit for the president to either sign, or veto, a bill.

But, let us look at it a moment. Nowhere in here does it actually give him the power to fully veto a measure, only to approve it as/is, or to return it with objections noted. As written, instead of the president being given a carte blanche to reject a bill, the president is being given the ability to subject objections to congress, who then can take up the changes. They can overrule his objections, or they can amend the bill to resolve the objections. This can be repeated until such time as the bill is either finally approved, or that the congressional session is finished. And if the president does neither, does not approve it or send it back with his objections, it becomes a law automatically after 10 days unless the congressional session is finished.

Rather than interpreting this as giving the president the power of veto, and instead that he is given the power of oversight, it changes the congressional dynamic by which the two branches function. It requires the president to be more engaged with congress, while also giving congress more avenues for bill approvals. This is, in fact, the original interpretation of this passage (as noted in Federalist #73), something which must be kept in mind as we explore.

Our current interpretation of once and done means that solid measures which just have issues, are rejected out of hand, or these issues which could be resolved through this back and forth amendment process are carried into law. It also means that the Legislature is partially immunized from the consequences of its own actions, and can pass a purposefully bad bill knowing that the President will stop it. Interpreting it such that no, the President cannot prevent a bill from passing, only suggest alterations which Congress must then take up, it puts all responsibility for said bills in the hands of our elected representatives.

This fits in with the Oligarch world view that the executive branch needs to be a powerful ruler, an emperor, who can act on their own. We need to reject it out of hand, and to restore the proper balance of the branches of government. Through the restoration of this interpretation, of this way of thinking about the role of both the legislative and executive branches of government, the People can have the government, have the nation, they deserve.

> *Every Order, Resolution, or Vote to which the Concurrence of the Senate and House of Representatives may be necessary (except on a question of Adjournment) shall be presented to the President of the United States; and before the Same shall take Effect, shall be approved by him, or being disapproved by him, shall be repassed by two thirds of the Senate and House of Representatives, according to the Rules and Limitations prescribed in the Case of a Bill.*

When both houses have to vote to pass a measure, it will require the executive of the nation to also sign it in order to pass, with only Adjournment being approved without the executives authority. This area has been bypassed with alarming impunity in cases where the congress and president are in disagreement. What is done is that congress labels this measure a "Concurrent Resolution" and claims that the measures were introduced independently, even if identical, therefore the presidential signature is not required. The claim is that since these resolutions do not have the force of law, executive approval is not needed.

This interpretation enables congress to engage in activities and behaviors which may not be to the benefit of the People. Through these measures, congress can create joint committees without the checks and balances required by the Constitution. They can start the budget process without presidential oversight. They can demand the return of a bill before signature. They are even used to pass measures to tell the president how congress feels on certain subjects.

In the 111th congress, there were many such measures put forward, which ranged from acknowledging the 150th anniversary of the arrival of the Sisters of the Sacred Hearts on Hawai'i to honoring former CNN host Larry King. In general congress wastes its time on pointless measures and not doing the needed work to keep the nation running, and this is one of the reasons why. By congress being given free reign to pass and approve measures without any check, they can and will waste time on hollow gestures in order to feel as if they are accomplishing something. That is human nature at work.

By interpreting this to include even these measures which do not have force of law, not only would it add a layer of approval to them, but when approved they would carry with them far greater value. Measures to honor service would now represent the government of the United States itself, not just one branch of it. Resolutions to accept donations for the capital rotunda would have the weight to demonstrate a true sense of accomplishment to them. Encouragement for foreign governments to release prisoners would then have the underlying notice that it was the voice of America talking.

It would also enable avenue by which communication and discourse can happen, by opening up avenues of agreement between sections of government which may be in opposition at the time. By limiting the approvals for honors being allocated for various anniversaries and notable events, it creates a wall between the branches which only has grown the disharmony between our branches of government. This change, while bearing no weight of law, helps to unify our government into a cohesive unit working for the common good – akin to trust building exercises performed by many enterprises elsewhere.

Section. 8.

The Congress shall have Power To lay and collect Taxes, Duties, Imposts and Excises, to pay the Debts and provide for the common Defence and general Welfare of the United States; but all Duties, Imposts and Excises shall be uniform throughout the United States;

While this may seem straightforward, this is one of the areas with the most diverse level of interpretation out there. You can find claims that this gives congress the power to tax, or that it denies their ability to tax. That this requires the payments of debt, or that debts don't count. That this enables to provide for welfare, and that it denies it.

As a result, this section will require a lot of breakdown.

Congress has the power to lay and collect taxes, duties, imposts and excises, in other words, to determine what will be taxed, and are charged with collecting it.

Now, this brings up an interesting point of the dynamic of our federal government.

While Congress, specifically the house, originates the bills to raise the revenue and are charged with collection, the task of actually collecting has been assigned to the executive branch through the Internal Revenue Service, an office within the Treasury Department.

Or rather, it has traditionally been assigned to the executive branch. There is no actual legislation making this an executive department, only that the President can remove the Secretary of the Treasury from office. It is not even specified here that the executive has the authority to appoint people to the office, or that they can make the approval for the removal. Only that the president does the actual removal.

Continuing, Congress is to pay the Debts of the nation. As demonstrated by the shutdowns, our congress is not following this as set forth in the Constitution. Additionally, later amendments further expanded upon this, which we will cover when we come to them. For now, this section requires our congress to deal with all matters involving the federal debt themselves.

By providing for the defense and welfare of the nation, the Constitution put forth that Congress was to preserve this nation, both from external and internal threats. Some those who would turn our nation into their own personal playground have tried to put that welfare, as described in this section, was some other animal from what we call welfare today, the truth is our modern welfare system began as a branch off of this original terminology.

Instead we must consider Welfare, and Defense, as we understand it today, not under some vague notion of what it may have stood for over 200 years ago. After all, back then, defense consisted of wooden ships, musket balls, and horses – why would we judge the other portion of this section, Welfare, by the same standard? It was claimed that the Welfare clause covered only taxation, but then why the pairing with defense? It is because the taxation is for the raising of revenue in order to fund defense and welfare, not that defense and welfare were for the purposes of taxation itself.

It also charges that taxation must be uniform throughout the nation. This is an area where our current interpretation is falling far short on.

Our tax code is complex, and heavily favors the wealthy, those who would serve as a petty aristocracy. This in turn produces an imbalanced tax code. In addition, our corporate system is so badly engineered that corporations can in effect avoid any taxes, even get tax rebates they did not earn. Ironically, our tax code is also very broad, with large umbrella structures such as Income Taxes dominating. And by being so broad, it invites complexity.

This is not a uniform system, but it is being interpreted in the same manner as claiming that handing everyone $100 is a uniform support system, regardless on what their actual needs are. It is uniform on an intellectual level, but not equal or equitable in any practical manner.

By interpreting it in such a manner, that uniform application is to be a strict numerical statistic rather than a relative designed for the particulars of each market, area, district or state, the Oligarchs have engineered a situation that creates haves and have-nots. This is unacceptable, for it then enables them to use the nuances of this design to create a shell game, exploiting every hole in the system in order to extract as much wealth and benefit from the People without paying back into the system needed to support them.

This in turn creates a disproportionate allocation of the general Welfare as demanded by the US Constitution. Instead of supporting the People, it becomes a tool to exploit. Rather than defending the People, it becomes the cudgel used to oppress. And it has to stop.

Let us consider this a moment. Right now, congress levies the taxes, but then does not collect them. Congress instead has the executive branch, through agencies such as the Treasury Department, handle the collection. This is not how it is structured in the Constitution. It charges for Congress to handle both the levy and collection. This does not mean the dismantling of the treasury department, the IRS, nor the federal reserve, as some would claim. It would mean a realignment.

There are no laws preventing the Treasury from operating as a Congressional Office. In fact, there is nothing preventing the Secretary from being the treasurer. While the president has to authorize any removal, as established earlier, resolutions to remove would require his signature regardless. By removing the politics from the position, we can turn the Treasury Department from being an executive appointment to instead a civic post. Even with the Treasurer remaining as part of the executive cabinet, it would be a reshaped role, one of stability in what is currently a very politically charged environment.

By interpreting this area as being one of equitable access, rather than flat access, combined with the use of the congressional officer portion of the Constitution can turn this area into a much more stable and less politicized system.

For one, congress cannot shutdown the government.

The Treasury, as part of the duties found within the legislative branch, would be tasked with executing the duties therein. The very notion of a shutdown would be nonsense, as the treasury would have the authority in place to do its duty. To stop it, congress would need to have both houses pass a measure, and the president to sign it. Otherwise, the Treasury Department would do its duty, as mundane and routine as it is, free from the politics of Washington D.C.

To borrow Money on the credit of the United States;

To further explore on the last point of the section above, through the positioning of the Treasury as a legislative, rather than executive, department, this becomes a simpler task. As of right now, Congress has to approve each and every borrow, even if they approved the spending bill requiring it, before the treasury can act due to the treasury being an executive, not a legislative branch. This causes the budget showdowns, the shutdowns, and the drama in Washington D.C. Through our adjustment, through seeing the US Constitution through our own eyes and not the eyes of those who would tear down our nation and dominate over it, we can revolve this issue directly.

With our interpretive adjustment, both the approval and execution exist within one body. Oversight remains a two-branch task, and the Secretary would remain a cabinet level position, but would work as civic office in much the same way as the Social Security Administration. This would in turn also give congress more general authority, even if not direct control, over the nations direction. After all, the power of the purse is strong indeed.

To regulate Commerce with foreign Nations, and among the several States, and with the Indian Tribes;

Trade is to be regulated by Congress. Like the Treasury, Congress has assigned this role to the Executive, contrary to what is written. The Department of Commerce, like the Treasury Department, needs to be relocated in order to not only fulfill the constitutional requirement, but also to better improve the department itself. Again, removing the political aspect, and instead turning into a civil officer under the legislative department, a level of insulation from politics is established. This in turn prevents the regular intrusion from outside influence who then use political contacts to compromise the departments ability to safely manage commerce.

At this point, the exercise should be clear that the top-to-bottom realignment of interpretation will reorganize not only the congress, but the division of powers within our government. Many of the ideas we hold to do not reflect what is written. And this means that we can adjust the way in which power in Washington D.C. is structured, how our government runs, and we can produce a far more accountable, far less politicized, system.

To establish an uniform Rule of Naturalization, and uniform Laws on the subject of Bankruptcies throughout the United States;

Here is a section which demonstrates an area Congress is granted the ability to delegate a role—they are to establish the rules and laws, but are not charged with direct management of these roles.

A uniform rule of naturalization has been interpreted in the past to mean that the specific naturalization process itself must be uniform – that all people must adhere to the same process of naturalization, but that it did not apply to the initial step in the naturalization process itself, that of entering the nation itself for naturalization. Again, per the current interpretation, we have equal application, but not equal access.

By shifting our interpretation to equal access it changes the dynamic for naturalization. Quotas by country are unconstitutional through this interpretation, eliminating the giving of favoritism to specific nationalities, to specific ethnic groups, or specific religions as we have now. This does not mean an open border, or unfettered immigration, but that the access itself must be uniform, not segmented as it is now. Adjustments can mean that immigration quotas must be handled per-need, or through a lottery system. Perhaps through a system by which sponsors in the US put forth the request to immigrate, rather than from the outside. Whatever system is decided, it cannot rely upon 19th century concepts of racial supremacy and Victorian era prejudices.

Bankruptcy is another area where our current system is not equitable. The requirement is for uniform laws on Bankruptcies, which has to-date been interpreted as having a uniform bankruptcy code nationwide. This is technically what we have, but the resulting system is not one which is uniform in its application.

Consider how the system unfairly targets the poor and the youth, while enabling the wealthy to rid themselves of any unwanted debt without any concerns. Right now, our bankruptcy code is not uniformly accessible, nor is it uniform in how it can be used once access is granted. Business debt can be removed without worry while students find themselves burdened with debt they can never hope to pay off. It needs to be structured to be uniform not in the letter of the law, but in how the People can use it. The bankruptcy code must be uniformly accessible and usable by the People or else it does not meet the requirements as set forth by the United States Constitution, per our interpretation.

To coin Money, regulate the Value thereof, and of foreign Coin, and fix the Standard of Weights and Measures;

Coining money, regulating its value, and the handling of foreign coin is at present handled by the Federal Reserve. Now, contrary to the opinion of certain people, the Federal Reserve is already an office functioning under legislative branch, which means no adjustments are required here. It functions above politics, helped by its members being handled much as civil servants and not political appointments. As a result, the Fed has avoided much of the jockeying you find in other departments.

Those who would seek to impose their will over us view this as a threat to their plans. By being independent of the politics, the Fed is difficult to manipulate by outside forces through Congress itself. By not being a unified structure, but 12 independent entities managed through a central board, it is even more difficult to directly influence. And it holds the power to regulate even the largest financial institutions, even holding the ability to completely shut them down. A very large threat indeed.

Instead of fearing the Fed, as those who wish to impose their own constitutional views upon us do, we should instead understand, and even strengthen its role in protecting the People. With the banking deregulation measures passed over the past few decades, freed from the regulations designed to prevent such consolidation, banks have learned to shop around between reserve banks, to get preferential treatment.

In the past, banks were limited to doing business within a reserve bank's district, so if a bank wished to operate in Missouri, they were limited to the St. Louis Federal Reserve. Now a bank which is structured under the Boston Federal Reserve can operate in Missouri. Eliminate this loophole, the various banks would become accountable to the regulatory body on the areas upon which they operate.

A win-win for all involved under this model interpretation, although we have stretched the definition of what we are aiming to do.

Now, one area we have forgotten about is the authority to regulate foreign exchange rates. At this time, we let private entities set this exchange rate, using a currency exchange market. This ability for private manipulation of exchange is precisely not what our founders desired, and in studying the modern world, it is an absolutely horrid idea. We are letting unaccountable, unregulated entities dictate our trade policies through currency trade manipulation. This is completely unacceptable.

Historically, the federal government kept a fixed rate of exchange, set in treaty, with foreign powers. We can witness the problems of a floating, market-based approach with the highly volatile fluctuations of goods. This makes things problematic for the people, who now are enslaved to the small group able to manipulate the currencies of nations. This needs to be restored, with the United States having a fixed, not a variable, exchange rate. As we can witness, the nations who keep a fixed exchange rate, such as the People's Republic of China, are at a trading advantage over those who do not.

To provide for the Punishment of counterfeiting the Securities and current Coin of the United States;

This has traditionally been handled by the Secret Service, a division of the Treasury Department. However, with the Department of Homeland Security, that division was relocated. What had been an enforcement arm with a few secondary tasks, the most notable of which is in protecting various elected officials and their families, became something else. Rather than breaking up counterfeit rings, the Secret Service has been modified to serve roles such as electronic criminal monitoring and expanding to overseas operations. Further, by being moved into the Department of Homeland Security, and the political jockeying which accompanied it, the division has had its independence from politics compromised. In recent years this has resulted in numerous security breaches surrounding various officials which they have protected.

It is by interpreting our enforcement arm of the treasury department as just another security group that this was allowed to happen. In so doing, it opens up this agency for the Oligarchs efforts to privatize roles of government. There has been considerable pressure to eliminate the department entirely, and to outsource it to mercenary companies such as Blackwater, now called Academi.

By restoring the Secret Service to its core role, that of protecting our currency, this threat to our nation can be averted. Part of doing that is to move it back to the

Treasury, now under the legislative branch, storing its role while further removing it from the politics which are interfering with their ability to do their jobs.

To establish Post Offices and post Roads;

One of the core duties of the nation is the establishment of communication, and of facilitating the democratization of communication. Directly, this applies to the post office, and the highways which support it. In the interpretation common today, this only requires that such post offices and postal roads exist, not that congress is to have any role in the management, upkeep or support of them, and that they are a narrow definition of both, explicit and limited.

However, the purpose of this was again to facilitate communication. The modern communication system is far broader than just mere Post Offices and post roads. Now we have a woven network, beyond just roads to include airports, telephones, the internet, etc. Interpreting this to represent the modern definition of the postal service, this would also require congress to establish, and therefore regulate, everything from airline service to broadband.

This is not a change of practical matter, but one of mentality. On all sides, there are calls to privatize all aspects of our civil service, of our societies root structure. We must remember that enshrined in the Constitution is the idea that our government is there to enable us to communicate between one another, not just to be a number for marketing agencies to sell product to. The Oligarchs would take away this foundation, these roots which hold us up, and make us beholden to them for the very things our Constitution was drafted to provide.

To promote the Progress of Science and useful Arts, by securing for limited Times to Authors and Inventors the exclusive Right to their respective Writings and Discoveries;

The oligarchs do argue that the government should not promote science, or art, and that the securing of rights should not go for to the authors and inventors but to the financial interests affiliated to them. This is part of their interpretation of the Constitution, that corporations, that capital itself, are people of equal or superior status to an actual person.

This interpretation has turned what was to be a method of reward into a program designed to exploit the People and enrich the burgeoning Oligarchy. This of course pleases the would be oligarchs, so they encourage the expansion of this as much as possible.

Instead, we need to ask ourselves, do we truly want to grant inanimate objects, pieces of paper really, rights and privilege that we ourselves cannot enjoy? No, we don't.

By stripping these artificial constructs of their personhood, this passage now can only interpret as referring to people directly. No, Big Pharmacy Firm, Inc did not invent that new wonder drug, it was Joe Researcher in lab B. By limiting who can benefit from invention to Joe Researcher, rather than Big Pharmacy Firm, it changes the dynamic by which these protections, namely Patents and Copyrights, can exist.

This is an area which will hit some of the most resistance, but it is one of the areas it is most critical to overcome the resistance. So long as we can grant a piece of paper the rights of the artist and inventor, then there is nothing to prevent that piece of paper from gaining other rights either. The dividing line needs to be clear, and absolute, and it must start here.

There will be those who claim that this will stifle innovation, but historically that has never been proven true. The idea of a corporation, and not a creator, having the right of patent or copyright is a new one. By interpreting this to only mean the direct human creators, be they a lone composer at a piano or a laboratory filled with scientists, technicians and engineers, we can begin to remove the oligarchs biggest strength – their ability to thwart competition and implement monopolies.

To constitute Tribunals inferior to the supreme Court;

In traditional interpretation, this is effectively limited to the setting up of the Federal Circuit Courts, and the Federal Appeals Courts. This is a gross under-utilization of the power granted here, for a Tribunal is a court, an arbitrator, a legislative body, administrative agency, or other body acting in an adjudicative capacity – anything with the authority to judge, adjudicate or determine claims in an official capacity. In other words, this can be expanded to offer more protections for the People from those who seek to enslave the nation.

Right now, administrative agencies, such as the Environmental Protection Agency, the National Forest Service and even the Department of Labor are given some room to regulate, but little power to actually give these regulations teeth. They apply penalties, fines, but lack any real strength to enforce. To have any real measure of penalty, they need to go to another whole department, the court system, and work their way through them. This puts them on bad ground from the beginning, as they are dealing with corporate lawyers who are well paid, and are trained to drag out court cases for long periods in order to force the government to settle.

In effect, the Oligarchs are exploiting the system as set up to prevent the government from doing its job effectively. Our founders could not have intended to set up a government which could not operate – why bother having a government in the first place? They put down the guidelines on how it was to operate.

By grossly misinterpreting what is written, by turning agencies from enforcers to mere tax collectors, the ability to punish those with wealth who break our laws is all but eliminated. And, a penalty to those with wealth which is just money, turns law adherence into a return on investment only. Does it cost more to follow the law or to break it? Considering the hundreds of billions lost in the recent banking scandals, with only pennies on the dollar in penalties for it, breaking the law can be very lucrative indeed.

To define and punish Piracies and Felonies committed on the high Seas, and Offences against the Law of Nations;

Here we find something interesting. To define and punish, pretty straight forward, but against the Law of Nations, that is something which needs to be explored, and remembered. The Law of Nations is actually a book, written in 1758 by Emerich dr Vattel, and applied to international relations. In the 18th century, this was a very thin subject, which made Vattel's work so monumental and influential.

Here, however, it is not limited to the book directly, and much of our current function of international law stems from this earlier book. It could even be stated that the United Nations is a growth from the seed Vattel planted so many centuries ago.

By this standard, the United States should be at the forefront in enforcement of international law. Instead, we find the US working very hard to avoid the international courts, to fail to punish those who violate the Law of Nations. At the time of the drafting of the Constitution, the high seas were the primary trade route, so adhering to international law was highly critical. Nations which failed to were ostracized, finding themselves cut off from trade goods.

The United States must adhere to international law, even when it would put ourselves at their mercy. Several nations have called for the US to hand over former leaders for trial as war criminals for their actions while head of state. How can we even dare claim to be a just nation, when we shield those who would make war against an innocent people?

That is not the America I was raised to believe in.

To declare War, grant Letters of Marque and Reprisal, and make Rules concerning Captures on Land and Water;

Congress, and congress alone can declare war, can set the rules which govern our nation in time of war, and grant approval for forces for use in war. But it does not have them commanding those forces – separation of powers between the branches of government.

But this section is a bit more interesting than that.

Letters of Marque and Reprisal are for the operation of privateers, ships in service to a nation not owned by the nation itself. Historically, this was used for pirate operations against enemy states, but not exclusively. The last such ship which was operated under such a letter was the Goodyear Blimp, Resolute, although it was not fully entered as such, having never had its letter signed by the president.

These however are capable tools for addressing specific needs. You can set these letters to fit specific targets, with specific rewards. Imagine, for example, the issuance of a letter for the capture of Somali pirate ships, or even open ended bounties, such as for the

FBI's most wanted list, enabling those with the ability to pursue the case without direct interference. It would give the US the ability to reach out in the world for security without the need for a massive military presence.

It can even be considered to cover foreign fighters working for the United States, an American version of the French Foreign Legion as it were. The French Foreign Legion is legendary, and during the colonial period incredibly effective in preventing uprisings. As the Foreign Legion used soldiers from many nations it generates a very different relationship with the local population. A multitude of cultures within the unit forces the soldiers to become culturally aware, and avoids many of the problems we find in the rank and file which are assigned to foreign lands.

But these are woefully underused. Instead of issuing letters where appropriate, the US tries to handle all such operations itself with mixed results. We now have had military bases in foreign countries older than the grandparents of those who serve on them. This is not the action of a republic, but of an empire. It breeds a military elitism, and is expressly warned against within the US Constitution itself. To handle these foreign operations, the Constitution leaves us with the Letters of Marque and Reprisal – to create independent but controlled entities tasked with specific goals as needed.

The Constitution also directs us to establish rules for capture, in effect rules of warfare. By establishing rules for capture, both on land and sea, this makes the way in which the US is to engage in warfare uniform. All agencies operating under Letters of Marque and Reprisal, must follow these rules. This is why the use of Letters is so important – it establishes a lawful keel for the nation. Consistent application of the rules creates regular results in our dealings with foreign leaders. By applying rules in an a la carte or haphazard fashion, those who we face at both the diplomatic table and battlefield cannot trust us to keep our word. We must stay the course with our rules of engagement, and apply them uniformly, be it against a man in uniform or against an insurgent.

Otherwise we have no moral leg to stand on.

> *To raise and support Armies, but no Appropriation of Money to that Use shall be for a longer Term than two Years;*

A nation cannot hide behind oceans, so an army of some sort will be required from time to time. In granting the authority to create an army, the Constitution put a rather curious phrase in place—*but no Appropriation of Money to that Use shall be for a longer Term than two Years.*

Now, in the common interpretation, this means simply that an Army is only to be funded for two years at a time. We witness this with the biannual passing of the National Defense Authorization Act. If this were so, however, the phrase should have been something closer to "and shall be Appropriated Money in two year Terms."

Instead of telling us the armies budget length, what this phrase is telling us that the use shall not be for longer than two years. As Congress is in command of the budget, this is incorporated here as well, to further restrict the operation of a standing army. In short, Congress can only issue the formation of a standing army for a period of up to two years, and they cannot issue out money for longer periods in order to circumvent this limitation through a per-purchase or allocation of funds.

What this does is to keep military tasks focused, and brief. Note, this does not mean that a military cannot exist, or cannot continue, but that it needs to be gated, termed, on a per-army case. To our founders, the army was not a single body, but instead was a multi-faceted entity. George Washington had an army in the Revolutionary war, but so did other generals. These were considered independent, although operating under a larger umbrella of the Continental Army.

This compartmentalization of the army is demonstrated later on, when the remaining regiments of the Continental Army were reorganized as the Legion of the United States. Each regiment was recreated as a mixed-force sub-Legion, and was itself an army. These armies, organized under the umbrella of the legion, operated under a two-year term. The Legion itself operated with stated goals issued by the President and authorized by Congress. These army terms were in rotation, and at the end of which Congress could decide if to renew.

History shows that Congress did let the authorization lapse for two of the Legion's units at one point, but recreated them later on when the British attempted to push back on the northern border in several incursions. Recruits were brought in together, trained together, and served together. The 2-year enlistment period seen in our current military is a carry over from this earlier period. By doing this, having these troops serve together from boot camp to discharge, it created a kinship between soldiers, and they became their own support system.

If a soldier at the end of the armies term chose to retire barring an extreme circumstance, they were free to do so without concern. If they chose to stay on, they became part of the training system for new recruits. Every new term, every new authorization, required a reaffirmation of their oath to protect and serve our nation, as set forth by the first US Congress on September 29, 1789:

> *I, A. B. do solemnly swear or affirm (as the case may be) that I will support the constitution of the United States.*

> *I, A. B. do solemnly swear or affirm (as the case may be) to bear true allegiance to the United States of America, and to serve them honestly and faithfully against all their enemies or opposers whatsoever, and to observe and obey the orders of the President of the United States of America, and the orders of the officers appointed over me.*

If a unit were to not be renewed, its members who wished to remain in service could of course petition to join one of the remaining units, who would then not require as many recruits to replace those retiring their service. This could result in an oversized sub-Legion from time to time, and Congress can address avenues for relieving this when it should happen.

As it is right now, the Army is made up of specialized divisions, which rely upon continual replenishment of soldiers. Organization happens at the top, and only the top, with the result that each division will eventually focus on the goal of retaining its position rather than on the longer term goals of the nation.

This is not a criticism, it is just an acceptance of reality. When a group has one goal, one purpose, one task, they will prioritize that to the exclusion of all others. Eventually, this group will behave in a manner to keep this task intact, even when it is no longer needed. When cuts happen, and cuts will happen, every group tries to push it onto another group – theirs is important, theirs must stay put. We witness this regularly with programs which serve no practical purpose.

By restoring this more classical interpretation, that an army is a single mixed-purpose unit, a legion, underneath the overall, civilian led, command structure, and could be renewed, or not, as a whole unit, we can eliminate this problem as well as eliminate a significant amount of bureaucratic overhead which plagues the military in the US.

Instead of a regiment being for infantry, or air support, or paratrooper, or armored cavalry, or engineering, each unit would have all of these. These legions would train, work, live, together, and operate as a team. This also means every soldier would have opportunities for parallel growth and the ability to be retasked when needed – and can then be used for far more purposes.

Imagine a new Legion of the United States for a moment, keeping the tasks which the US Army today does handle. In a natural disaster, the ways in which an existing unit can be used are limited, but in a mixed-role legion, we find far more capability even with less manpower. A paratrooper may serve as firefighting support, a tank driver may operate an ambulance, a sniper can serve as a lookout or spotter, the possibilities grow and change as we explore this.

And as the unit now does not serve any single role, it becomes simpler to wind up, or down, as needed. In times of war, new units can and will be needed. In times of peace, they need to be set aside.

As it is, we have a problem when it comes time to set aside our swords – our politicians are forced to increase military budgets even during peacetime else be attacked as not supporting our troops for elections. By having a standing army, only requiring budget lines every two years, rather than a commissioned legion, we perpetuate this cycle, and our military spirals out of control.

By focusing on the Constitution, and its call for a renewal of the army every 2 years, it all but forces the need for such a legion structure, and our founders understood that.

To provide and maintain a Navy;

Compare this to the earlier requirement for an army, and it is clear that unlike the Army, with its two-year term, a Navy was viewed as a continual need. Letters of Marque and Reprisal are needed, but would never sustain the nation which relied upon sea trade as much as we do.

By keeping this simple rather than the more complex phrasing found with the armies above, this sends a message pure and simple – the Navy is essential. Congress is ordered to provide, and maintain a navy. This means Congress is directed to order ships, to organize their crew, to issue directives, and to maintain the men and material needed for the Navy.

This grants a lot of leeway, but at the same time, the US Navy is less of an issue than the other branches. It can, and has, been drawn down, putting ships into mothballs until needed, several times over the past few hundred years. Many ships built for WWI and WWII were put into these mothball "Reserve Fleets" for either later use, or scrap.

The wisdom in not limiting the Navy to a term is then held in this fact, that unlike an army, the navy is far more flexible and easy to manage. A long standing army is difficult to disarm without a fixed schedule, while a Navy can be drawn down with fewer entanglements due to the nature of the military branch.

In addition, the US Navy offers ground combat soldiers as well, the Marine Corps. Formed originally in 1775, the Continental Marines were specialized sailors used for boarding enemy vessels. After the war, there remained a handful of these Marines, part of the newly formed US Navy. In 1794, with a worry over a potential war with France looming, Congress ordered the building of new naval vessels, each one outfitted with a unit of Marines.

These soldiers serve as our direct presence when the US needs to project force, such as during the First Barbary War. Having such soldiers, attached to the Navy, means less ground troops are actually needed for our defense. Being attached to highly mobile operating environments, ships, the US can bring them where they are needed, when they are needed.

After all, the alternative for troop deployment is to have soldiers sitting in various locations in case something happens. This means a far larger force is required, and such an army, a force not as mobile, is harder to maintain in general. Combining this focus of a naval based fighting force with the 2-year term given to land armies, this then demonstrates that our Constitution was frames for a more flexible military model, one better able to adapt to change, to being scaled up, or down, as the demand is there.

Something to consider, however, is that in the era that the Constitution was written, the idea of an airborne military unit, or even one able to reach the vacuum of space, was nearly impossible to even conceptualize. As a result, to some minds, this could mean that the US can have no air force. Our founders would not have accepted that, and if you consider the Constitution carefully, we do not need to either.

The Air Force is a standalone organization for the United States. This is not the only way in which it can be organized – many militaries around the world have their air combat divisions as part of a larger organizational force. The US used to have this, with the United States Army Air Forces as well as the US Navy and Marines both operating their own air units. The reason it was split into its own division was mainly due to politics at the time, and the belief that all of the US's air power would eventually be folded in to this single department as we find in nations such as the United Kingdom. History has shown that did not happen, the result of lobbying between the various branches.

With a restoration of the Legion concept, the termed operation of armies, we can move this air power back to the Army. As these armies would be independent, but coordinated from a higher office, this makes it quite possible to make it easier to coordinate between army and navy as well – let us be honest, we would have less brass to let their egos get in the way.

To make Rules for the Government and Regulation of the land and naval Forces;

Notice here that this is held up independently of the rules for capture given prior. This denotes that the armies and navy are to have additional rules and regulations beyond the general engagement put forth in the Letter of Marque section. This means that Congress and Congress alone designs the structure, organizes the systems, regulates the material. They may not command the forces, but they determine what these forces can do.

As it is, we let our own militaries or the executive branch make these decisions far too often. This is not a viable system – as discussed earlier, these agencies eventually focus on maintaining their positions, maintaining their budgets, and avoiding any cuts rather than focusing on the task at hand. This is why the United States is currently retiring older carriers, to validate the construction of brand new supercarriers. So far almost a half-dozen vessels, including the iconic USS Enterprise and USS John F. Kennedy, have been placed into reserve, or are being prepared for life as a museum or for scrap.

To validate the construction of new vessels, we find the retirement of existing ones, even if the demand for new is not there. We are currently operating with a navy of just over 400 vessels, higher than we had only a decade ago. And this rapid growth is without a viable naval threat against us. And it happens because of this system we have in place, enabling the lobbying for position in the budget.

It needs to end.

To provide for calling forth the Militia to execute the Laws of the Union, suppress Insurrections and repel Invasions;

Read this again a moment and ponder. Many out there would claim that the Militia stood with the states, as a counter for federal aggression or overreach. But in the Constitution it clearly states that Congress is to call forth the Militia. But, what it can call the Militia for, that is where things take a bit of a turn. It must be noted that the Militia itself is not defined here, only the roles in which it is to serve. We must deal with an interpretation, or rather, the interpretation as the founders understood it and then adapt it to fit our modern times.

In the colonies, and in Britain at the time, the Militia was a group of volunteers, local citizens who had two roles – posse comitatus, an assembly put together by a law officer for the apprehension of lawbreakers, and the fyrd, an informal military body designed to serve as the last line of defense of a shire. Comparing with what powers the drafters of our Constitution reserved for them, it is clear that they were not diverging from the classic British model.

As described here, the Militia is for three purposes, executing the law (posse comitatus), suppressing insurrections and repelling invasions (fyrd). Since the establishment of a navy and army has been handled earlier in the Constitution, the use for an invasion is less than one might consider. So, as that is last, and can be considered the least needed, one would be wise to use the three areas in order of priority, of importance for the Militia.

So, this would mean that a Militia's first role is that of executing the Law – acting in the role we today give to a variety of officials ranging from police officers to court bailiffs. At the time the Constitution was written, the idea of a uniformed, formal police force was unheard of. Indeed, the first police force was not implemented until the 1800's. Instead, law enforcement fell to a variety of individuals, such as the Watch, who were volunteers, Sheriff's who were elected, or Constables whom were appointed by city governments or courts. Many were untrained, or poorly trained, and the capability to uniformly execute the laws varied from town to town, and even from block to block.

This inconsistent law enforcement system was problematic for the early nation, so Congress aimed to rectify it by organizing these separate elements under the auspices of the Militia. Rather than relying upon a formal law enforcement officer, such as a Bailey or Sheriff, the Constitution tasked the Militia to execute the laws of the Union, that is laws passed by local, state and federal governments. Combine this with the earlier requirement for documenting and publishing all laws, and we have the foundation for a uniform code of justice in this country.

The next portion is in the handling of insurrections. At the time, the United States was dealing with regular incidents between British loyalists, Spanish incursions, French nationals, and the native tribes. Having an army, even a large one, would be pointless against these small unit actions. They could not respond in time, and would be difficult to manage against adversity so small and mobile, so instead the use of the Militia was ideal. These events would be far less frequent than the need for law enforcement, so it is a lower priority within the Constitution for the Militia.

Insurrections also could occur from other citizens as well, which Shays Rebellion was a fresh reminder for our founders. Contrary to the popular cultural representation put forth today, Shays Rebellion was not a mob of poor farmers, but was instead a collective group of anti-government radicals from all socio-economic levels. Its root cause ultimately boiled down to the lack of a uniform federal monetary or legal standard.

At the time, the United States was functioning much as 13 independent nations (14 if you considered Vermont, who had broken away from New York, but was unable to join the United States due to the limits of the Articles of Confederation). The currencies between these nations were inconsistent, and merchants refused to take the various colonial bills.

In Shays Rebellion, what ultimately stopped the insurrection was not an army, but a local militia organized by Benjamin Lincoln. Organized by democratically elected committees, paid for by donations by over 125 merchants, this militia forced the insurrection's leaders out of Massachusetts. Then when they tried to invade from neighboring New York, the militia, which had appeared to have disbanded, reformed almost immediately and put an end to the rebellion once and for all. With this event fresh in their minds, the drafters of the Constitution formalized this very role for the Militia. We find this role filled today by modern police departments as well.

Lastly, the Militia is to serve for defense against invasion. The Revolutionary War was still fresh in peoples minds at the time, so the idea of an invasion was quite real to the drafters. As they had already established a navy, and the basic structure for a federal army, this last role was added not as an afterthought, but as a last line of defense. To serve the earlier two roles, organization is required. This organization could then be turned for a final defensive measure, one last chance to push off an invasion from hostile forces.

By formalizing it here, it creates the trifecta for the role which the Militia is to fill. The Constitution does not isolate these three areas, but demands that those which serve for one, must serve for all. That those able men and women who were to defend us from invasion were also expected to execute the law, and to put down insurrections if needed. This requirement puts a lot of pressure upon the Militia, they need more training than just a simple handling of a rifle at a range against a paper target. And that is addressed in the next section.

But this triple role also creates another structure as well, one of society's wardens. The Militia is made of the People, which means that those who are to protect your homes are your friends, your family, your neighbors, yourself. You do not have some nameless man in a dark suit with a badge and a gun show up when the police are needed, you have your neighbor arrive to handle the situation. Rather than taking some teenager graffiti artist to jail, the official here has another option, to talk to the family as friends and neighbors. In other words, the People are treated like adults, and expected to manage themselves in most cases.

And as your neighbors are there to protect you, both from the breaking of the law as well as more serious threats, they have more incentive to do the right thing. The person who responds, who enforces the law, has the responsibility of the role, but is not a full authority themselves. This means you stand equal to them, for they are you as well. It forces a cooperative resolution. By having the people do the initial policing themselves, by keeping it within the neighborhood, much of the antagonism and conflict we have witnessed these past few decades, especially with the militarization of the nations police, can be addressed in a healing manner.

This does not mean that there is not a role for professional police officers, but it does change the nature of this role. Instead of being the first line of defense, of handling the petty tasks and disturbances, they become the overseers and the investigators – constables in the classical sense. As the United States uses a British court system, with equal opposition with an arbiter, instead of an investigational justice system as we found in the Kingdom of Prussia, this need for a unit divorced from law enforcement to handle the investigations that can and will be needed is critical. This division of roles means that now the police are not a universal law enforcement group, but would serve in this investigational role as well as managing this overall militia structure.

Recall that the militia is there for law enforcement, but were not granted the powers of the court for things such as arrest, the issuing of citations, handling of warrants, etc. This specialization of role for the police helps prevent the abuse of authority we often find troubling major cities in these modern times. Also keep in mind that earlier Congress was granted the authority to enforce regulations directly as well through tribunals. The militia would be but a part of a larger legislative engine, one tied first to the communities from which it draws its volunteers.

This divorce of power enables a proper set of checks and balances to take place. As it is right now, the police have universal authority of law enforcement and investigation. Due to the nature of these roles they have to work closely with the court system. This makes oversight of any issues, be it corruption, abuse, etc, difficult if not impossible. The legendary thin blue line prevents much internal dissent, and the courts which oversee them also depend on them for both revenue in the form of citations as well as validation in the form of arrests. It is actually against the prosecutors, against the courts best interest to manage the police as a result. By divorcing this responsibility, and putting direct enforcement under a unit regulated by the legislature and not the courts, it introduces the chance for checks and balances in to the system.

When you put power in the hands of a single group, the chance for opportunism, and corruption increases. Too much power, the risk grows larger. By splitting law enforcement, by adding this independent layer to the legal process, one which is engineered to be only local, to be neighbors supporting neighbors, it diffuses the power significantly. This also creates a layer of local standards for law enforcement. If a law is seen as unjust by the citizens it is there to protect, it will be harder to enforce due to these local enforcement groups. And if an act is seen as criminal, but no actual law exists to resolve it, there is an immediate feedback to the legislative process to have it addressed.

> *To provide for organizing, arming, and disciplining, the Militia, and for governing such Part of them as may be employed in the Service of the United States, reserving to the States respectively, the Appointment of the Officers, and the Authority of training the Militia according to the discipline prescribed by Congress;*

With the understanding of the role in which the Militia will play comes then a delegation of authority and responsibility for it. Rather than a pure allocation of authority to Congress, or to the states, the Constitution split these responsibilities up according to a very specific formula.

For Congress, the order is to handle organization, the armament and setting the standards for discipline. This way each militia would be uniform, made to meet the same standards, use the same equipment – uniformity where it makes the most sense. But it is the areas not prescribed to Congress which tells us more of how the Militia was envisioned to work.

The first thing states are charged with is the appointing officers and handling the training of the Militia, all to the standards set by the federal government. This is intentional on several levels. The officers, in our interpretation Police Officers rather than military, being appointed by the state, rather than the federal, government means that the officers would themselves, while not necessarily neighbors, would have a higher probability for some affinity with the local militia members and the conditions found in their neighborhoods.

The other role assigned to the states the actual duties of training. This keeps the militia a local, enforcement, force, rather than a national force able to project the will of the United States. While Congress prescribes the structure, and handles the overall supervision and regulation of the militia, the states can better determine their training criteria and focus. After all, a Virginia militia has far less need for volcano preparedness than would Washington state's militia.

This setup demonstrates that the Militia, unlike the armies, navy, and marque'd groups, is entirely focused on domestic, regional issues. It is not designed to be the sole defensive force for the United States, with defense from invasion their last, not their first, duty. Instead it is intended to be the last line of defense against foreign threats, and the first line of defense for domestic tranquility.

Yet, instead of this role for the Militia today, we find a military organization. Contrary to some claims, the Militia still exists. No, it is not those guys who go into the woods on weekends to shoot up military style weapons. The militia today is organized under the Office of National Guard. While it does serve in the latter two roles, the first, and primary role of the Militia has been long forgotten.

It was re-organized this way after the Spanish American War, when the US attempted to use militias for foreign operations. This was not their intended role, but a half-century of interpretation that the militias were to be the sole army, when the Constitution expressed a different role, caused significant issues for the United States. By attempting to use 150,000 militia members as regular soldiers, valuable time and energy was wasted. While some units, such as the 1st New Mexico under Lt. Colonel Theodore Roosevelt (later to become president) did take notable actions in the war, the vast majority were so underskilled, and ill-equipped that they never left their training camps.

Rather than addressing the issue by focusing on the regular army, the government at that time decided to militarize the militia. At that point, the idea of a public police force, rather than the militia, as the first line of law enforcement was long established. This was a result of the civil war when militias nationwide were diverted to handling the insurrection of the south, forcing towns and cities nationwide to hire professional police officers. By the time the war ended, the local militia night watch and constable were long forgotten, a scar from the trauma from the war which set brother against brother.

Combining these ideas, the Letters of Marque and Reprisal, the termed armies, the navy with its marines, and the militia along with the Rules of Capture, we can get a clear impression as to what it is our military should look like.

What we find is a tiered system, one with a delegation of role but designed for the parts to support and compliment each other. The use of Letters of Marque enables the creation and execution of tasks without the dedication of resources, the use of rewards for private addressing of our concerns where needed. Our Navy works as a fast deployment unit, projecting our presence where needed worldwide, but with no significant domestic support capability to speak of. The armies serve as a backbone structure for domestic defense and can serve as well for some projection when the goal is well established, not ideal for quick operations but when a goal is set does the job admirably. And the Militia is for handling domestic needs, a police force as well as last line of defense in case of invasion, not for a specific goal or any remote projection – local application only.

It is not a military for imperialism, but one which reflects a value system of domestic strength with worldwide support and respect. It reflects a humbler nation, but one which knows how to prioritize its values. By separating out its military power, the Constitution details out a balanced approach to military strength.

> *To exercise exclusive Legislation in all Cases whatsoever, over such District (not exceeding ten Miles square) as may, by Cession of particular States, and the Acceptance of Congress, become the Seat of the Government of the United States, and to exercise like Authority over all Places purchased by the Consent of the Legislature of the State in which the Same shall be, for the Erection of Forts, Magazines, Arsenals, dock-Yards, and other needful Buildings;—And*

A government needs a place to govern from, and the authority to have such a seat of power is found here. It is not however exclusively for just locating the seat of the government, it also covers the control over it, and other federal buildings or property which the government may need, mentioning those of a military nature while not limiting it to such. The framers who wrote the Constitution could not know what manner of buildings or property would be needed in the future, so they left much of this open ended.

What it did do however was to put a size limit on what the federal government could use for the nation's capitol – 100 square miles. This provision grants Congress has the right to legislate and control directly the territory within which the seat of government is located – what we today call Washington D.C.

However, this section continues past just the selection of the seat of government, and addresses other territories which the federal government may need control over. As stated, this gives Congress the authority over all places purchased by the federal government as well. Purchase of territory by the federal government must happen with the permission of the state within which the territory is located – so no buying up huge tracts of New Jersey without that states legislature and governor signing off of on it.

The requirement for a states permission before purchase of territory contained within it is a preventative measure. While the only territory owned by the government with exclusive administration is Washington D.C., the federal government does administer all other territories owned as well, even if not in an exclusive manner. A state may not wish to have an armory located next to a hospital, for instance. This enables the state to decide how much, or how little, federally administrated territory to enable within their borders.

This of course does mean that territory not within a state is fair game. Our purchase of various pieces of territory over the years, such as Alaska and the Louisiana Purchase, attests to the use of such tactics for expansion of the nation. Of course territory owned before a state came to be, such as huge sections of Nevada for example, would be under no such restriction as well.

As it is, the section grants a broad ability to purchase territory as needed, but with the needed check and balance for power. Contrary to some claims, this does not limit the federal government to being only effective within the District of Columbia, a form of

Vatican City isolate from the rest of the nation. It is clear here that the federal government is to maintain facilities, to own territory, and to administer them.

But what of territories owned by the United States? Do the citizens of those territories have rights as well? As clearly stated within later amendments, yes, they do. The problem comes in that they are not given full autonomy, as a state would be. Note how the District of Columbia lacks full representation within Congress.

We shall explore their potential later on.

> *To make all Laws which shall be necessary and proper for carrying into Execution the foregoing Powers, and all other Powers vested by this Constitution in the Government of the United States, or in any Department or Officer thereof.*

Here is where the authorization for enacting these policies is granted. Having the principle is fine, but without action they are meaningless in a practical sense. This is a directive is for Congress to enact the legislation needed for fulfilling these commands, preventing them from sitting on their hands and not implementing one or more.

It does more than just this narrow group of policies either however. It specified that Congress must make law as well for the *"necessary and proper"* execution of *"all other Powers vested by this Constitution in the Government of the United States of in any Department or Officer thereof."* Here is where we enter new territory.

Earlier, the Constitution granted the formation of tribunals, which can create, manage and implement the regulations necessary for their office. Now we have a section whereby Congress is to make law the powers vested by these tribunals and offices. Under the current interpretation, this is Congress gets to set down the law, and the offices act accordingly. But that is not how a tribunal works. It is set forth with a task, given a mission, and is there to fulfill it until no longer needed. And indeed, if a tribunal rules in such a way as to make a law required in order to fulfill their appointed duty, Congress is obliged to pass this law.

Right now, to gain experts on a topic for the creation of a law, Congress finds lobbying agencies and private groups ready and willing to provide portions, or even full laws. These laws often times are biased, poorly done, full of loopholes, or easily exploited – as befitting those done by private interests.

This interpretation, that Congress is to pass laws made by the various federal agencies, means another avenue for the creation of laws currently missing – that of experts unaffiliated to private monied interests. This avenue grants a new way for legislation to be drafted, and passed, by those with the most experience on a subject. As it is right now, these departments many times have their hands tied by the lack of legislation, or worse, contrary legislation to their appointed duties. As they are currently limited only to execution, this is to be expected.

But here, it clearly states that these offices are part of the drafting of laws, rather than just victims of them. Rather than committees which can be the victims of political maneuvers, partisan politics or attacks on policy by legislators who are beholden to fundraisers for elections, we have these offices, the agencies themselves, enabled to draft these laws for the legislature. The legislature of course can amend, or reject such laws, as is their right, but the advantage of letting those who are most familiar with the subject at hand draft the law proposals is something we cannot ignore.

So far we have not found any text or description which would enable private entities to directly draft laws. What we find is an express list whom may draft laws: The House of Representatives, the Senate, as well as the federal departments, officers and tribunals.

Section. 9.

> The Migration or Importation of such Persons as any of the States now existing shall think proper to admit, shall not be prohibited by the Congress prior to the Year one thousand eight hundred and eight, but a Tax or duty may be imposed on such Importation, not exceeding ten dollars for each Person.

At the time the Constitution was drafted, this was considered a measure regulating slavery, a promise that the importation of new slaves would not be prohibited before 1808, with a tax or duty levied accordingly. However, it is not exclusive with this, which means that the section does actually still apply in some manner or fashion.

The use of the term Migration or Importation gives us a clue for other avenues for use, and how we can use this section to address other issues we are currently facing – namely that of foreign migrant workers.

At this time, our nation is facing an issue of foreign migrant workers, people who come to this country to work for a time before returning to their home nation. We currently process them on the federal level as immigrants, even if they are not immigrating to this nation, but only traveling for work. This creates a load on the system which hurts those who do wish to move to our nation.

If we stop viewing this section as for slaves, but instead for any importation or migration purposes, this opens up new avenues to relieve pressure on the immigration system. It specifies that congress is allowed to limit the importation and migration of people, but directs the states for managing this function. It also limits the amount of tax or duty that the federal government can levy on this role to no more than ten dollars.

So, let us use this approach, and grant states the power to handle worker permits, limiting those migrants to those states. States set their quotas, states handle entry and exit processing, with the federal government only setting absolute, national limits. This enables each state to better asses and manage its direct needs. And by having the states manage entry and exit for these migrated or imported workers, it keeps the federal immigration system from becoming overworked. Division of labor where it is most logical.

Rather than trying to deal with the labor market for a whole nation as a single entity, we would instead have this divided into 50 individual elements. In theory, the ability to focus on their immediate labor market demands should simplify the process for migrant workers. These workers would be limited to labor within their state of access, and the state would then manage the handling of those who overstay their permit of entry directly.

This would also put penalties not on the workers, but on the companies which hire them. Since now migrant workers would incur a tax upon the business, failure to follow the law would hit the business in the pocketbook. A few financial penalties, tax liens upon some larger businesses, and the system would quickly self regulate.

This would also limit imported labor to a geographical area. A workers permit would only apply for their labor within a geographic area, while they could move freely otherwise.

The Privilege of the Writ of Habeas Corpus shall not be suspended, unless when in Cases of Rebellion or Invasion the public Safety may require it.

Habeas Corpus, Latin for "that you have the body," is one of the founding principles of the United States legal system. It is used for bringing a prisoner before the court to determine if their detainment is lawful. This here states that no person can be detained by the United States, or any courts which work under the jurisdiction of the United States, without being held for being charged with, or convicted of a crime, or for some other lawful measure such as being a prisoner of war or for safety purposes as prescribed in law.

Congress has been granted here the authority to suspend the writ in cases of rebellion or invasion, for the good of public safety, and that is it. However, if you analyze the application of habeas corpus, it is not in full effect. Congress in 1789 ordered its application only for federal cases, with this expanded in the civil war to also enable federal courts to grant relief to state prisoners using it.

However this was later overturned in legal challenges. Courts found that it needs to apply on the state and local level, as well as in any projection of the United States, such as on a naval vessel or foreign base of operations. Otherwise it becomes useless, and legal exploitation of the system to deny the legal protections granted by our Constitution is trivial.

The purpose of Habeas Corpus is in putting the onus on the federal, state, county and local legislators for being clear in the letter of the law in the handling of criminal cases. If something is not specified out in law, it cannot be enforced. This prevents arbitrary application of punishment, or the holding of a prisoner indefinitely without them being notified as to why they are being held.

Several restrictions put upon the Writ of Habeas Corpus, such as a statute of limitations, the denial of access to federal courts by those in military custody, and the denial of access to even file a writ until after state avenues have been exhausted, goes against the principle of this portion of the Constitution. This is the area in which focus is needed, where flawed principles and ideas must be addressed. This privilege, this right, is needed, and is the foundation for our entire concept of legal rights.

No Bill of Attainder or ex post facto Law shall be passed.

A Bill of Attainder is the arbitrary conviction through legislation, that is without the privilege of a judicial trial. Ex post facto, Latin for "from a thing done afterward," is the application of retroactive punishment, to render something criminal after the fact and then apply punishment for acts taken before the law was passed. This prohibition put upon Congress is there to prevent punitive applications, or for the legislature, and not the courts, to arbitrarily decide upon a persons guilt.

Historically, Bill of Attainders were for the seizure of property from a criminal, in order to deny it from being passed on to his or her heirs. This became a problem due to the use of overuse and exploitation, as authorities used them to mete out punishment without due process. Kings used it to steal property, to eliminate potential rivals, or to simply eliminate the civil rights for a group of people arbitrarily. Sadly, the use of them is still found in the United States today, through actions such as mandatory sentencing laws for criminal cases.

Ex post facto is to prevent a legislature from declaring something criminal in order to punish someone for having already committed the act in the past, when it was legal to do so, or when it was a less severe penalty for it. This does not mean that laws without retroactive effects are prohibited, mind you. This has been decided for a long time to apply to criminal, not civil matters, starting in 1798 with Carter vs. Bull.

No Capitation, or other direct, Tax shall be laid, unless in Proportion to the Census or enumeration herein before directed to be taken.

Contrary to popular belief, the 16th Amendment did not overturn this provision of the Constitution. Those who claim it was do not understand what a Capitation is, or is not. A Capitation is a levy based on a uniform amount per person. In medicine, this amount is for physician payment, where you pay the same amount on a regular basis for medical care. In education it is an additional fee to cover expenses collected from students. In this case, it would be a uniform tax levied against all people within the United States who meet a set requirement.

This provision simply puts that any such uniform per-person tax cannot be levied unless tied to the census. This is to make sure that any such taxation is uniform among all citizens. This may be tied to a service, such as the telecommunications tax, but it still must be handled through direct, equal proportion. No punishing California citizens with a higher tax rate than Wyoming, for example.

This was judged by the supreme court was not applying to a personal income tax, requiring a special amendment to enable such. But it can apply to other taxes and fees none the less, as demonstrated by levies on everything from land use to cable TV.

No Tax or Duty shall be laid on Articles exported from any State.

One of the issues found under the Articles of Confederation was the imposition of taxes, or duties, between the states. It created barriers of trade which hurt the nation as a whole, creating pockets of industry with few incentives to work cooperatively. For the nation to grow, it needed industry. Industry needs resources. Many times, the right location for industry is not where resources can be found. Such barriers created added cost of doing business, and over time added up to a large drag on the early economy.

By itself, this provision is relatively simple, without the need for much exploration, but it is tied to the next provision, and once combined there is a serious issue afoot within the United States, one which is undermining our national unity, and hurting our economy.

No Preference shall be given by any Regulation of Commerce or Revenue to the Ports of one State over those of another: nor shall Vessels bound to, or from, one State, be obliged to enter, clear, or pay Duties in another.

This is an area where we have states which are skirting the intent of the US Constitution, driven by the business oligarchs who play states off of each other in order to cheat their way out of taxes and revenue owed.

On the surface, this is a simple statement to prevent the states from imposing a tariff or other duty between each other, or from imposing a unique tax, duty or tariff which benefits one state over another. However, there is a small element which does come into play, namely the word "Preference." None is to be given, but the truth is, preference is given constantly, through the use of tax incentives designed to lure businesses from one state to another.

If we hold up that these incentives to lure a business from one state to another are indeed preferential treatment for trade, we find ourselves with a double standard forming. For things which stay within the United States, these programs are perfectly constitutional. However, for those which then are tied to exports, or for a business which imports from another nation, then many of them are indeed unconstitutional. No Preference must be given, which applies to both the federal government, and between the states themselves.

If a state lures a business using a tax incentive, credit, or payment, and the business deals with exports or imports, then that state has created a preferential tax or duty, clearly in violation of this portion of the Constitution.

By limiting such incentives to domestic use only, these incentives can and many do generate growth. However once it begins dealing with imports or exports, it quickly becomes a race to the bottom as states start lobbying against each other to lower the bar, quickly causing revenue shortfalls or unfair tax systems that hurt the nation as a whole.

By putting a hard cap on programs, that any who take advantage cannot import or export goods and services, it puts an end to the widespread abuse of our tax system by international entities. It also immediately puts an end to many forms of tax shelters, which rely upon international operation and relocation to create the loopholes through which money is funneled to the oligarchs and out of the people's hands.

No Money shall be drawn from the Treasury, but in Consequence of Appropriations made by Law; and a regular Statement and Account of the Receipts and Expenditures of all public Money shall be published from time to time.

For money to be spent, Congress needs to sign the appropriations into law. All expenditures need to be accounted for. But this is more than just a section authorizing what is in effect a large ledger.

Not only do expenditures need to be recorded, but the receipts, the evidence of what we have procured with the money spent, must be published. Our fathers did not trust secret programs, black operations which were kept hidden from the treasury, and neither should we. Now, this does not mean that we cannot have spies or counter-intelligence, for all nations do engage in espionage, but that we are to engage in it with a more honest approach.

Rather than appropriations being listed under code names, we list what it is they are doing, even if the subjects are not revealed until later. After all, the publication is not immediate, but time-appropriate. Of more immediate is the record of monetary expenditure, with the key information as to details to be released later, when it is no longer of strategic concern to our nation to keep it under wraps.

Of course, a time limit needs to be applied. We cannot have programs which would so outrage the public that the release cannot be within the term of a sitting Senator. That is three congressional terms, three budgets. Programs which are that secret are programs which undermine the United States itself, our way of life and what we stand for as a nation.

No Title of Nobility shall be granted by the United States: And no Person holding any Office of Profit or Trust under them, shall, without the Consent of the Congress, accept of any present, Emolument, Office, or Title, of any kind whatever, from any King, Prince, or foreign State.

The use of noble titles to create a tiered society has a long history. Part of the goal with one is to create an incentive system for reinforcement of class strata. Those who serve to the benefit to the elites get rewarded, while those who do not get oppressed. It is the antithesis of democracy and the republic which is the United States of America.

But this is far more than just a title of nobility, it covers a wide variety of areas. In addition to a title, which is prohibited to all US Citizens without approval of congress, other areas which are prohibited for office holders of the government include being granted an office, given a present or an Emolument. It is this last element which is of special importance here.

One of the biggest issues our nation is facing currently is money in politics. And much of this money is earned overseas, thanks to the global economy. In other words, most political contributions are emoluments, prohibited by the US Constitution except by special dispensation granted by congress on a case-by-case basis. Imagine having to vote on each contribution by a wealthy donor for any race, be it federal, state or local. It is doubtful that congress would agree to it, so all such donations must be rendered null and void.

But how does one determine is donations are domestic or foreign? The simple truth is, one can't easily. The ease of shell companies, of outside action groups, laundering foreign money into domestic purposes, renders even domestic donations suspect. The only way to adhere to this provision in a reasonable and fair manner is to ban all outside spending, all donations, to political campaigns and those running for office.

Section. 10.

No State shall enter into any Treaty, Alliance, or Confederation; grant Letters of Marque and Reprisal; coin Money; emit Bills of Credit; make any Thing but gold and silver Coin a Tender in Payment of Debts; pass any Bill of Attainder, ex post facto Law, or Law impairing the Obligation of Contracts, or grant any Title of Nobility.

Here is where we find the states being limited in their powers under the Constitution. The powers enumerated above for the federal government now are being denied to the states, granting the federal government oversight and command of the nation as a whole.

One section is notable for a historical standpoint—States are denied being able to create treaties, alliances, or confederations on their own. It was this provision which made the Confederacy of the American Civil War illegal. Even that the southern states made a confederacy among each other, it is forbidden under the Constitution for them to have done so.

On currency, the use of the phrase gold and silver Coin refers of course to the Spanish "piece of 8" system which was universally accepted in the New World at the time. The English word for a piece of 8 was the Dollar. While the terminology here is old, it refers directly to the dollar as the mechanism of currency to be used within the United States.

And there are provisions here which prohibit action for both the federal and state governments. No passing of laws which apply retroactively, no applying a punishment to a group and not a person through law, no titles of nobility, etc. This is to again keep a logical, and stable, system of government for all people throughout the United States.

No State shall, without the Consent of the Congress, lay any Imposts or Duties on Imports or Exports, except what may be absolutely necessary for executing it's inspection Laws: and the net Produce of all Duties and Imposts, laid by any State on Imports or Exports, shall be for the Use of the Treasury of the United States; and all such Laws shall be subject to the Revision and Controul of the Congress.

This prevents states from imposing their own taxes or tariffs on imports or exports. Recall earlier how tax incentives are in effect such a levied tax, this is the area which makes the use of tax incentives for businesses themselves unconstitutional under such an interpretation. These incentives are to be revised, and controlled by congress itself, according to this.

The lack of such oversight has resulted in states actively lobbying against each other in the attempt to draw businesses to their state. And such programs are behind the continuing erosion of revenue throughout the nation, as trillions of US dollars now sit overseas and unable to produce domestic economic growth. But this is how the oligarchs wish it, to "starve the beast" as it were. By playing states tax codes off of each other to their own advantage, the hope is to disrupt the essential functions of government and in so doing to create a utopia for themselves by denying it to the people.

> *No State shall, without the Consent of Congress, lay any Duty of Tonnage, keep Troops, or Ships of War in time of Peace, enter into any Agreement or Compact with another State, or with a foreign Power, or engage in War, unless actually invaded, or in such imminent Danger as will not admit of delay.*

Again, we are witnessing how the states are being divested of the powers granted to the Federal government. While the States are granted control over the Militia, they are denied control over the Navy and Army. They may not negotiate treaties, or settle peace accords.

What has now been set up is a clear dividing line between State and Federal. The Federation which is the United States (properly a Federal Republic) becomes the framework by which it interacts with the world. While the State governments are their own internal authority, they have no actual power in the world itself. The Federal government is given full authority there.

When people discuss States Rights, they often times do not understand what it is that States Rights actually are.

In 1832, South Carolina attempted to claim that States Rights enabled it to nullify the tariffs on imported goods. This claim fell apart as clearly the Constitution as written denies them this, specifically stating that international commerce is excluded. And nowhere is the concept of "Nullification" found.

The Civil War was in many ways a battle of States Rights. The Confederacy however was fundamentally flawed here, in that even had they won, it would have been a loss. The very nature of the rebellion would have resulted in a complete dissolution of the Confederacy within a generation. The only reason it held together for the few years it was is due to the external Union to focus upon. If left alone, it would have fragmented, and dissolved in short order. It almost happened as it were.

Another area of States Rights has been that of civil rights, that a State would claim it could grant or deny the rights guaranteed within the US Constitution at will. This is once again not a solid position, for if a state could dictate to the Federal on the rights of citizens, then there was no structure for the government of that state to dictate from in the first place. The same framework which granted the rights to the State government was also that which granted the citizenship rights, so to undermine one would undermine the other.

Indeed, history now has told us that when the term "States Rights" is used, it is inevitably to mirror some capability which the person themselves disagrees with, and not any actual authority granted in the US Constitution.

You rarely if ever hear anyone discussing States Rights over an actual power expressly granted to the states, after all. When was the last time you heard someone bringing up the States Rights issue over the ability to organize property taxation, or on the ability to set highway speed limits?

The push for what is often termed "State Sovereignty" is little more than an attempt to undermine, and dismantle, the US Constitution itself. It is a seditious and potentially treasonous act, and one that should not be taken as flippantly as it appears many are want to do. Nullification is unconstitutional, as is declaring the State a sovereign.

Be wary of those who would call for States Rights, Nullification or State Sovereignty, for they do not act as good stewards of this great nation, and would sooner see us dismantled than accept their civic responsibilities given as a Citizen of these United States.

Article. II.

Section. 1.

The executive Power shall be vested in a President of the United States of America. He shall hold his Office during the Term of four Years, and, together with the Vice President, chosen for the same Term, be elected, as follows

To execute laws, executive power is needed. Unlike other nations such as the United Kingdom where the legislative and executive power is shared, the United States made the purposeful division of this power. This is part of what is called "checks and balances" as any good civics student is aware.

By doing this, the goal is to prevent any one group from having complete control over the government. It is also set that the President's term is longer than that of a Representative, but less than that of a Senator, striking a balance between the two at four years.

To support him, the Constitution once again brings up the Vice President, mentioned prior as the leader of the Senate. By having the Vice President with overall management of the upper house of Congress, this was to give the people a direct say in who controls the avenues of legislation. But, by only being to the upper house, and not the lower house which handles the procurement and allocation of funds, there is no single person who can force through financial measures – a key ability easily abused by anyone.

Currently, we have the power of both Head of State and Head of Government invested within the President. But this is not inherent even with how the Constitution is written. Our traditions make it so, and our traditions only. Because of this division, of President and Vice-President, with the Vice-President in the upper house of Congress, we have multiple options by which we can improve our government, all though interpretation, the biggest improvement being the divorcing of these two segments of power.

Each State shall appoint, in such Manner as the Legislature thereof may direct, a Number of Electors, equal to the whole Number of Senators and Representatives to which the State may be entitled in the Congress: but no Senator or Representative, or Person holding an Office of Trust or Profit under the United States, shall be appointed an Elector.

This creates what is now called the Electoral College. You will note, the words "Electoral College" are not used, but that is the traditional name for these electors. How they are appointed varies from state to state, and what they can cast their vote as is similarly unique. Regardless of their own selection, these electors are the direct voting apparatus for the election of the president. In most states, the general voting population for that state select these electors, who in turn elect the president. For most states, they must vote as a single block, using First Past the Post methodology, also called Winner-Take-All.

There are those who would argue for dividing the electoral votes up by districts, but this then only makes the system susceptible to gerrymandering, changing the problem as it stands for a new one which we already know as a failure. This only encourages further disenfranchisement of the electorate. Vote rigging is rewarded, while honest elections become nearly impossible. This proposed solution is as bad, if not worse, than the problem it seeks to address.

As such, there are few options for resolving this, but options are there. We can either push for more direct systems for electing the President. We can move to a more Parliamentary system with party based appointments. We can even move to an indirect election system which would make the President more of a manager than a ruler. The options before us need to be explored.

And again, we still have the Vice President as the head of the Senate. This means we have avenues to explore, and the interaction of these two is critical to that.

> *The Electors shall meet in their respective States, and vote by Ballot for two Persons, of whom one at least shall not be an Inhabitant of the same State with themselves. And they shall make a List of all the Persons voted for, and of the Number of Votes for each; which List they shall sign and certify, and transmit sealed to the Seat of the Government of the United States, directed to the President of the Senate. The President of the Senate shall, in the Presence of the Senate and House of Representatives, open all the Certificates, and the Votes shall then be counted. The Person having the greatest Number of Votes shall be the President, if such Number be a Majority of the whole Number of Electors appointed; and if there be more than one who have such Majority, and have an equal Number of Votes, then the House of Representatives shall immediately chuse by Ballot one of them for President; and if no Person have a Majority, then from the five highest on the List the said House shall in like Manner chuse the President. But in chusing the President, the Votes shall be taken by States, the Representation from each State having one Vote; A quorum for this Purpose shall consist of a Member or Members from two thirds of the States, and a Majority of all the States shall be necessary to a Choice. In every Case, after the Choice of the President, the Person having the greatest Number of Votes of the Electors shall be the Vice President. But if there should remain two or more who have equal Votes, the Senate shall chuse from them by Ballot the Vice President.*

This section has now been replaced by later amendments to the Constitution, so we will not go much into detail. The original model is for each elector to cast votes for at least two people, of which one cannot be of the same state as the elector. This model in turn would prevent a single large state from dominating the executive branch. If a tie were to occur, then it would fall to the House of Representatives to vote for who would be President, and the Senate for Vice-President. Only someone who had taken 50% +1 could take office, forcing revote after revote until a winner was reached.

For those who belong to a proportional parliamentary system, this system likely would sound familiar. But unlike those parliaments, where the core functions of government would continue while the elections were resolved, the United States would be frozen until the election of a President and Vice-President. Many nations have an autopilot mode, so that their social systems would continue working even while the government itself was organizing itself. Ours simply does not.

But this is not the only way in which this can be interpreted. Our current system is the result of Andrew Jackson and his efforts to win the presidency. His belief in direct democracy led us to our current interpretation of the President to be elected by popular vote, although through the legacy of the Electoral College.

However, as this section has been altered by later Amendments, even this interpretation is already rendered obsolete.

> *The Congress may determine the Time of chusing the Electors, and the Day on which they shall give their Votes; which Day shall be the same throughout the United States.*

The idea of a single nationwide day for elections is founded right here. By establishing such a nationwide day, it was to prevent the very "first in the nation" issue which now plagues our primary system.

Primaries have set in as the primary competition for any office. Due to gerrymandering, the number of competitive districts is virtually non-existent. But this in turn makes primaries now the true bastion of competition.

Primaries within the First Past the Post election become in effect a run-off, to narrow a lot of choices down to two. However, by tying these to the parties, rather than functioning as a run-off, as it did in the past, it gives undue power to a handful of people.

By rigging the system to avoid competition, the parties can indeed protect themselves, for a few elections. In reality, the competition simply moves up the chain – From election day to primary day.

The failure here is the very idea of a primary day as separate from election day itself. The Constitution is clear, elections must be held on one day. By splitting this vote, between primary and election, we have undermined the very power granted by the Constitution. By the use of the First Past the Post election methodology, while allowing two parties to dominate the two slots it necessitates, it becomes a recipe for disaster.

Having a primary and election at once however is difficult if not impossible to handle in a practical manner. Therefore it can be argued that primaries themselves are unconstitutional. And without primaries, the very structure of a First Past the Post election is itself unsupportable under the Constitution.

This means that for elections of the President, a different system is required.

> *No Person except a natural born Citizen, or a Citizen of the United States, at the time of the Adoption of this Constitution, shall be eligible to the Office of President; neither shall any Person be eligible to that Office who shall not have attained to the Age of thirty five Years, and been fourteen Years a Resident within the United States.*

Contrary to some radical thoughts out there, the phrase natural born citizen refers to someone who is, functionally, a living person. It was held in opposition to an artificial person, or corporation.

The distinction has been lost in modern times, when artificial people are given the rights of a natural person (IE *Citizens United*). A restoration of this interpretation, that the rights of people apply only to natural born and not a corporation, is needed for so many reasons.

If we took the Citizens United decision to the logical conclusion, a corporation could get married, run for political office, even count on a state's census record. So, re-establishing what is in the Constitution, differentiating between a Natural Born and an Artificial person, is needed.

In Case of the Removal of the President from Office, or of his Death, Resignation, or Inability to discharge the Powers and Duties of the said Office, the Same shall devolve on the Vice President, and the Congress may by Law provide for the Case of Removal, Death, Resignation or Inability, both of the President and Vice President, declaring what Officer shall then act as President, and such Officer shall act accordingly, until the Disability be removed, or a President shall be elected.

While this particular section has been augmented by later amendments, it is still important to pay attention to what it is that the founders anticipated. The Vice President, in addition to being the head of the Senate, also is the person who replaces the President in case he leaves office.

Clearly the founders did not want the selection of a President to be done ad nauseum. New parties rise to power, remove the sitting President, put their own person into the top office. So, they made the selection of his replacement as part of the process for selecting the President in the first place.

This has since been altered through Amendments, so exploring this and giving the alternative interpretations shall be done there.

The President shall, at stated Times, receive for his Services, a Compensation, which shall neither be encreased nor diminished during the Period for which he shall have been elected, and he shall not receive within that Period any other Emolument from the United States, or any of them.

As with Congress, the President is compensated for his time in office. Also as with congress, the President's pay is not to be increased, or decreased during his term. This may seem obvious, but during the 18th century, the idea of holding someone blackmail by withholding their paycheck if they were to vote against some legislation was quite real. Also, bribing them by offering a pay increase if they were to agree to some bill or another was also a real concern.

However this can be more broadly interpreted to include campaign contributions. After all, donations would be considered compensation under the broadest interpretations. Therefore, in order to be constitutional, political donations, or the claim that money is speech, is not supported by the Constitution through this interpretation. Even public funding would be unconstitutional, and campaigns would then have to use the commons, and nothing else.

Imagine a campaign season without annoying attack ads, billboards, and signs littering the landscape. Politicians would be forced to engage with the people directly, using news programs and outlets to get their message across. And, in the grand old tradition, the stump speech and public debate would become once again all important.

Before he enter on the Execution of his Office, he shall take the following Oath or Affirmation:—"I do solemnly swear (or affirm) that I will faithfully execute the Office of President of the United States, and will to the best of my Ability, preserve, protect and defend the Constitution of the United States."

During the 18th century, Oaths had far more weight than we give them today. The verbal agreement had weight of law behind it after all. By including the Oath within the Constitution, they limited and specified what duties they expected the President to perform.

According to the Oath, the President is to execute the role which the Constitution and laws allocate to the office of President. The President's other task involves protecting the Constitution itself.

However, as currently interpreted, the President also is the foremost interpreter of the Constitution following the Supreme Court itself. This means that preserving, protecting and defending the Constitution falls heavily in to the President's view of the Constitution.

That is not the way in which a functional system can operate. Changing the rules of the game with every election only would make all of the rules, all of the laws, meaningless. Yet this is what is happening now.

A preservation of standing, a continuation of policy, is what our founders expected, and what we need. Yet it is not what we have. The divorcing of Presidential position from legislative oversight only makes such a split, where the President goes from a continuing operation to an episodic nightmare of regulatory red tape. Every new election means effectively new rules, and it becomes impossible for us to plan for the future.

Section. 2.

The President shall be Commander in Chief of the Army and Navy of the United States, and of the Militia of the several States, when called into the actual Service of the United States; he may require the Opinion, in writing, of the principal Officer in each of the executive Departments, upon any Subject relating to the Duties of their respective Offices, and he shall have Power to grant Reprieves and Pardons for Offences against the United States, except in Cases of Impeachment.

When defining the role for the President, the first role is for the national defense, be it Army, Navy or the Militia. As established earlier, the Militia's first role is for law enforcement, which in turn means that the President is to oversee the execution, and enforcement of laws as part of his duties.

This would maintain our current Justice Department directly under the President. While most other departments and offices would be moved to the Legislature, law enforcement remains a more active and preventative than regulatory role, so maintaining its current arrangement becomes critical. However, by removing areas of distraction to the executive, this refocus on law enforcement would in time lead to a better overall system of justice.

Beyond this, he is to gain advise from the heads of the various departments, a role we now call the Cabinet. When the nation was founded, it was unknown how this particular role would be executed. It was President Washington who organized the officers of the departments in to the cabinet we know today.

We have already discussed moving the cabinet departments from the executive branch to the legislative. Directed by the Vice-President in his role of President of the Senate, this move would alleviate some of the responsibility of the president, empower congress, while alleviating the roadblocks which currently cripple our government. This would function in much the same manner as with the President's consultation with the Senate, but in a more direct manner. The President would still attend cabinet meetings, but now would no longer be running them. Instead he would be there for purposes of consultation, and for clarification of how to properly execute the tasks before him.

As part of his duty as the executor of law enforcement, he is also granted the power to grant reprieves and pardons for any offense short of impeachment. Over the years, this has been interpreted such as to cover not just pardons, but also commutations of sentence, remissions, respites and amnesties. This power is not only welcome, but needed for the President to be capable of faithfully executing the role of office and his duty as the primary law enforcement officer of the United States.

And by serving as oversight, with little direct power, the risks of Executive overreach and abuse of power are, if not mitigated, at least reduced. By the cabinet's functions becoming civic, rather than political, offices, it should also help make corruption and abuse far less probable, while also reducing its impact.

Consolidation of power into a single office is dangerous, as numerous other Presidential systems of government collapsing into dictatorship demonstrate. We are not a parliament, but this does not mean that we cannot adapt ourselves so as to reduce our own risk in the future, while retaining that uniquely American system of governance.

> *He shall have Power, by and with the Advice and Consent of the Senate, to make Treaties, provided two thirds of the Senators present concur; and he shall nominate, and by and with the Advice and Consent of the Senate, shall appoint Ambassadors, other public Ministers and Consuls, Judges of the supreme Court, and all other Officers of the United States, whose Appointments are not herein otherwise provided for, and which shall be established by Law: but the Congress may by Law vest the Appointment of such inferior Officers, as they think proper, in the President alone, in the Courts of Law, or in the Heads of Departments.*

The President and the president alone is given the power to make treaties, to handle international affairs, with the Senate only advising and granting consent of them once concluded. The reason for this is quite basic – to prevent a conflicting foreign policy. As the Commander-in-Chief, the President handles all foreign affairs of a military nature, while this role, as chief Ambassador if you will, makes his role handle the other side of that coin, diplomacy, as well.

For fulfilling this duty, the President is granted the authority to appoint ambassadors. As well, he is to appoint ministers, consuls, judges and all other officers. These are to be voted on by the Senate for approval.

Remember, Officers were listed in Article I as the head of legislative offices and departments. In effect, the President is to appoint the heads for these departments.

This may seem odd, but it makes a certain level of sense. By having the offices function as part of the Legislature, but with management and oversight by the Executive, it avoids a lot of the issues we currently are witness to with our executive-only offices.

Note how it is Congress which may create the inferior offices, and manage the appointment of those who work within them. Clearly, they cannot vote on every single office worker, but the creation of a bureaucracy with the goal of managing based on Congressional guidelines is clearly the end-goal.

One area of dysfunction we have had as of late is the holding up nominees using procedural moves. Which brings us to the next section.

The President shall have Power to fill up all Vacancies that may happen during the Recess of the Senate, by granting Commissions which shall expire at the End of their next Session.

When the Senate is unable to vote on a nominee, the President can have them fill the role until the next Senate session. The goal was to prevent vacancies from crippling offices.

To prevent these recess appointments, the Senate has enacted a lot of strange rituals, such as calling into session without any members in attendance. This falls victim to the quorum requirement set earlier in the Constitution. If there are not enough members in attendance to hold a quorum, it cannot be considered in session, and becomes a de facto recess. Yet, it is now routine for just such acts to happen.

This is not a functional form of governance, and undermines the roles both of these branches of government are there to fill. Instead of acting as a check on each other, in order to keep balance, the result is instead roadblocks getting in the way of governance, which we have seen in full effect these past several decades.

After all, if an office is not functional, it hurts the basic functions of government.

Section. 3.

He shall from time to time give to the Congress Information of the State of the Union, and recommend to their Consideration such Measures as he shall judge necessary and expedient; he may, on extraordinary Occasions, convene both Houses, or either of them, and in Case of Disagreement between them, with Respect to the Time of Adjournment, he may adjourn them to such Time as he shall think proper; he shall receive Ambassadors and other public Ministers; he shall take Care that the Laws be faithfully executed, and shall Commission all the Officers of the United States.

Let us split this section up some, as it covers a lot of territory in very few words.

Giving Congress information as to the State of the Union is a multi-pronged avenue. The most visible of this is, of course, the State of the Union address. In it, not only does the president give an address, but also provides the next portion of the section –

Consideration of Measures. The chief executive lays out a plan of action, alongside covering the status of the nation. While this does not need to be done in a speech, with several Presidents opting to instead send a letter, it is most often given as a speech before a joint session of Congress.

Beyond this, the President also runs an informational office as part of the executive suite of powers, the Governmental Publishing Office. Founded in 1861, it took over for the Public Printer, an informal office which had existed since the founding of this nation. The Public Printer was a contracted position, with Congress assigning the contract to the publishing house with the lowest bid. The result from this approach of contracted, private printing is that the governmental record from this era is incomplete at best, with no records from the floor of the Senate existing for year-long stretches.

The GPO enables the president to regularly supply updates to Congress, giving them regular insights as to the state of the nation, the results of programs enacted, and to suggest proposals to Congress itself.

However, the second half of this, to recommend proposals, has so far been interpreted for many years as to mean little more than giving wishful thinking or ideas. The President was not to submit actual legislation for consideration is a common thought. It is also historically wrong. Presidents have written legislation. Historically, we have interpreted the earlier passages such that only a member of Congress can submit a piece of legislation. But, by our earlier opening up the submission of legislation to people who are not a direct member of Congress, we now find that the President and the cabinet officers can, and should, be able to submit legislation, and amendments, directly to Congress.

This change by itself changes the dynamic between the two branches. Combine with the earlier changes, the two branches of government are forced partners. Neither can function without the other, nor should they function without the other. But, let us continue, for the remainder of this section further reinforces this partnership.

It clearly states here that the President may convene the Congress during extraordinary circumstances. The most obvious of these would be President Franklin Roosevelt's convening of Congress in the wake of the attack on Pearl Harbor. But other circumstances can arise, and should Congress fail to do its duty, such as failing to fund the government, would qualify for such a situation. Imagine some rogue Congressman attempting to pull off another shutdown, and then not be allowed to leave.

This also enables the President to adjourn one or both houses of Congress, should one or either refuse to do so. This power, the power of dismissal, does not attach any limitation of extraordinary to this power. The President can, in effect, force Congress to shut down, sending the members home, if needed. If the President were to force Congress to stay in session, any attempt for one to adjourn would empower the

President to adjourn both.

Now, recall the earlier discussion on a President's power to make recess appointments. Combine that with this ability, and it is clear who the founders wanted in charge of office management was the President, not Congress. The current antics of holding office nominations hostage is the antithesis for what makes a functional government.

The President also is to receive public ministers and ambassadors, solidifying the role as the point-man in foreign relations. As the President appoints our ambassadors, and receives foreign ambassadors, they become the gateway for our relationship with the world. This role is balanced against the Senate, who have the authority to approve treaties (which the President would negotiate) and against Congress which is allowed to advise the President in foreign matters, but not to interfere.

This is very important a distinction to make. Treaties are long term documents, and would affect our nation for decades or more. The negotiations to make such documents however are highly sensitive, and outside interference can, and will, destroy them. We only have to look to the collapsed Vietnamese peace talks of the 1960's, caused when future President Richard Nixon interfered with the negotiations and as a result the war not only continued, but escalated. This was as intended by Nixon, but is directly in opposition to what the Constitution laid out for us.

Both the President and Congress need to keep this division of role in mind. Too often, we have Presidents ignoring the advise of Congress, or Congress meddling in negotiations. And we have the issue of treaties labeled as "Trade Deals" in order to bypass the super-majority vote needed for approval. This is not what was intended, nor is it good governance.

Recall the earlier provisions for delivering information to Congress? In order for Congress to advise, they need information. The President should, on a regular basis during such negotiations, issue informational updates to Congress, let us say once a week on Monday. Then, Congress has 5 days, until Friday, to issue its advise based on that information. Make this a scheduled program, not this willy-nilly farce it is today where negotiations are in secret and interfered with. A simple bill outlying the process would vastly improve matters, and put into place punishments, such as censure, for violations.

The President is charged to "Make Care that the Laws be Faithfully Executed" as part of his duties. This is part of the continuing underlying issue of our executive branch, where the President fails to enforce, or even acknowledge the law.

Clearly our founders knew that this could be an issue, which is why their model put the offices under the Legislature, rather than the Executive. Under that arrangement, if a President were to refuse to faithfully execute, the functions of government would operate in a sort of autopilot. However, as time went on, these offices were migrated over to the executive, resulting in the President's current ability to be faithless.

If restored to the Legislative, there could be a conflict in power, unless we also took the earlier mention of the Vice President as the President of the Senate as quite literal, and moved his position also over to the Legislative. At no point does the Constitution state that the Vice President was part of the Executive branch, it must be noted. Instead, all of his powers are listed within the Legislative section of the Constitution.

As it is today, the Vice President directly oversees the executive offices for the President. This would continue, only which branch is ultimately in charge would change. If we greatly expanded the Vice President's role, combined with his management of cabinet offices, the Vice President would now function as the Head of Government, in the same role as the Prime Minister in a Parliamentary system. No longer a "spare" for the President, an empowered Vice President would shape policy, and manage the Senate.

With the depowering of political parties as we seek, this role becomes very important indeed. The Vice President would be replacing the Leaders of the Senate, as it were. The Whips would now be reporting to the Vice President. Which legislation the Senate picks up would be decided by the Vice President. The migrated legislative offices would, when combined with this role, prevent the forms of governmental breakdowns which now plague our nation.

Also, by divorcing the role of Head of Government from the President, it would prevent the potential for a dictatorship to form. By a President containing the full powers of Head of State and Head of Government, the avenues through which power can be consolidated are many. Divorcing them, empowering the Vice President, would help bring the government back into balance.

Even then, the potential for the abuse of position exists for either role. Fortunately, the Constitution includes the tool by which Congress could hold these offices accountable.

Section. 4.

The President, Vice President and all civil Officers of the United States, shall be removed from Office on Impeachment for, and Conviction of, Treason, Bribery, or other high Crimes and Misdemeanors.

Unlike Congress, which oversees itself, the President is clearly under the oversight of Congress. The oversight is split between two roles, described earlier, of Impeachment, and Conviction. Without both, no civil officer can be removed from office. This is to help prevent a simple majority in one house from playing politics with policy.

But as it is put into Congresses hands, if and when a President fails to follow the law, Congress can, if of single voice, hold the high executive accountable.

The problem comes when politics enters the picture. A political vendetta against a President could turn very ugly, and once the power is abused, it becomes far easier to abuse again in the future.

Party politics once again is the bugbear, once again the flaw in the system. When a political party becomes a gatekeeper, it becomes far too easy to fall into party-line thinking. Anyone not of the party is the opposition, therefore to be eliminated.

Empowering the Vice President now puts a roadblock on such action. As we will read later, the Constitution clearly empowers the Vice President to serve as a breaker both against Congressional abuse as well as against Presidential overreach. Through the movement of the Vice President from executive to legislative role, and taking steps for reducing party power in politics, we can restore the balance to our system of government.

This necessitates the divorcing of election tickets, however. No longer would the President and Vice President be running in partnership, but be independently elected items in the same election. While they would have the same electors, in theory, this divorce on the ballot is necessary to make clear the weight of this shifting in power.

For without restoring this balance, the system put in place as a last resort becomes a target for removal by those seeking to break our system of government.

Article III.

Section. 1.

The judicial Power of the United States, shall be vested in one supreme Court, and in such inferior Courts as the Congress may from time to time ordain and establish. The Judges, both of the supreme and inferior Courts, shall hold their Offices during good Behaviour, and shall, at stated Times, receive for their Services, a Compensation, which shall not be diminished during their Continuance in Office.

The Supreme Court was created to be the third branch of the US government. The framers of our constitution used a different model than that of the British by making the judiciary independent of the legislature. One proposed Constitution, by Alexander Hamilton, retained the unified legislature/judicial system, but was passed over in favor of our triumvirate approach.

By separating the judicial functions of government from the upper house of the legislature, our founders aimed to make a legal system which was independent, and accountable. It would be charged to operate within a framework, which is a uniform set of standards – from the highest court of the land to the lowest all courts would be held to the same level of scrutiny and oversight.

And as with the other branches, the founders set that the justices shall not have their pay cut. The fear of having the coin purse used as a club to force decisions remains a real issue to deal with today.

Section. 2.

The judicial Power shall extend to all Cases, in Law and Equity, arising under this Constitution, the Laws of the United States, and Treaties made, or which shall be made, under their Authority;—to all Cases affecting Ambassadors, other public Ministers and Consuls;—to all Cases of admiralty and maritime Jurisdiction;—to Controversies to which the United States shall be a Party;—to Controversies between two or more States;—between a State and Citizens of another State,—between Citizens of different States,—between Citizens of the same State claiming Lands under Grants of different States, and between a State, or the Citizens thereof, and foreign States, Citizens or Subjects.

This gives the Supreme Court their purpose. The court is set up to handle virtually all legal cases. This in turn makes the Supreme Court the final say on any question regarding the constitutionality of a law.

Of note, one section, between a state and citizen of another state, has since been amended, and is no longer enforced.

In all Cases affecting Ambassadors, other public Ministers and Consuls, and those in which a State shall be Party, the supreme Court shall have original Jurisdiction. In all the other Cases before mentioned, the supreme Court shall have appellate Jurisdiction, both as to Law and Fact, with such Exceptions, and under such Regulations as the Congress shall make.

The founders viewed the Supreme Court as being the first court in dealing with public officials as well as those involving the state government itself. For all others, it was to be a secondary. Over time, this was refined into our appeal process.

But a key element in here is long forgotten, that the court is regulated by the Legislature. The Constitution gave Congress the ability to set Exceptions, and Regulations, over the court. The scope of this has never been fully explored, or defined, but remains in place.

But this can be an area of development. As of right now, the justices sitting on out highest court of the land face an issue of corruption. One justice alone, Clarence Thomas, has, through his wife, been granted over a million dollars from groups which had cases before him. This is where Congress needs to step in.

There exist a series of rules on lower court justices to prevent these kinds of conflicts. The easiest solution would be to accept those as applying to the highest court in our land as well. By doing so, justices with clear conflicts can be recused.

The other issue we face is that every Supreme Court case is weighed in by all Supreme Court justices. This makes recusals difficult to accept, for it would leave any court case a justice short.

At no point does the Constitution require the full membership of the court to listen to every case. A simple solution would be that each Supreme Court case would not have a full court hearing it. We have 9 Supreme Court justices, it would be simple enough to have a small sub-group of these 9 hear and decide upon each case, say 3. Then, when there is a case of conflict, the case would not be short a justice to listen and weigh in.

These two steps, to enforce the regulations on the lower courts upon the highest and the use of a justice panel to hear the case and not the full court, it would enable the largest issue of our court to be resolved. But the final piece of this is in how the Supreme Court accepts these cases to begin with. Not every case can go to the court. Four justices must accept the case to be heard. Four justices, removed from nine, gives us five.

The four justices who accepted the case to the court would therefore be removed from the pool, leaving us the remaining 5 for justices to hear the case. Of those five, only 3 would be able to hear it, giving us two on standby should there be need for recusal. This then makes a two-stage Supreme Court, and helps prevent the abuse we have found so often today.

Of course, the court can overrule these 3 if so desired. A full vote, with a super-majority of 6-3, would then be used to overrule the active judges from the case. This then becomes a check of power. Add to it a standard for overruling at a super-majority, we create a court system designed for the prevention of politicized court decisions.

> *The Trial of all Crimes, except in Cases of Impeachment, shall be by Jury; and such Trial shall be held in the State where the said Crimes shall have been committed; but when not committed within any State, the Trial shall be at such Place or Places as the Congress may by Law have directed.*

By making all crimes to be evaluated by a Jury save those of Impeachment means that ultimately, all decisions are made by the people, not political appointments. Also, by requiring cases to be tried within the state of offense, it prevents district shopping.

Both of these are critical to a fair application of law. If a law is unfair, the jury is empowered to nullify it. When a case is moved away from where the crime occurred, it becomes far easier to manipulate the proceedings. The Constitution clearly tells us here that court cases need to appear before a Jury, not even just a Grand Jury.

Our current legal system has all but abandoned this. By some reports, over 90% of all convictions never reach a Jury. This turns these convictions into show trials of the truest sense. Without the Jury, they have no legitimacy, per the Constitution.

Some will argue that the Jury process slows down justice, but that is the point. Punishment of Crimes is not to be taken lightly, that our legal system is not to render every little possible offense as a crime. Create too many laws, your court system becomes bogged down.

This is a preventative measure, one deceptively simple by design. If any nation rendered itself dependent upon a prison population, it would lose its legitimacy. A prime example is the current war on Drugs, which has rendered the legal system a circus. By the treatment of illness as crime, we now have surpassed even the Soviet Union for histories largest prison system.

Recall, our law enforcement is to be handled by the militia, in other words, the People themselves. Then consider that our justice system also has the People inserted as well to serve on the jury. This is not an independent system, but two sides of the same. At every point, the People, you and I, are to be the final arbiters of what our laws are to stand for.

And lastly, the ability of Congress to decide upon where court cases dealing with extra-state territories is found here. This is surprisingly needed, with the amount of foreign territory the US operates bases on. The trial by Jury and use of Militia for law enforcement however remains, so this becomes a way for territories and protectorates to be covered without needing a neo-feudalistic nobility of oligarchs.

This comes up with an issue however. As it is right now, the United States Congress does not at this time give our territories full rights. However, this section clearly shows that rights are to uniform. As a result we have a whole group who have been denied full citizenship. The People cannot operate under such a system.

Our territories and protectorates need to operate under the same laws and enforcement as the rest of us. Otherwise, the People will be abused by those we elect, and our power will be slowly eroded. For when we can extradite someone to some out of the way territory and deny them full rights, we all are at risk.

Section. 3.

Treason against the United States, shall consist only in levying War against them, or in adhering to their Enemies, giving them Aid and Comfort. No Person shall be convicted of Treason unless on the Testimony of two Witnesses to the same overt Act, or on Confession in open Court.

An unusual measure, the metric for Treason is laid out very clearly. It can only be done in times of war. If a citizen of the United States is part of an enemy force, or gives Aid and Comfort to an enemy force, they can be found guilty of Treason.

But just when they define them, they then put a strict restriction upon it. The act must be overt, that is not hidden. It also requires direct witnesses to that act, or a confession. And even then, this is further restricted, and it cannot be a confession to a judge, a police officer, but in open court.

Remember, open court would include the Jury, made up of the People. The confession must be to them, directly. Merely confessing the crime to the police, a judge, even live on national television, would be insufficient. It must be direct, to a gathered Jury tasked with this duty, to count.

With Treason given such a high metric, it is no wonder it is so rarely applied, even when justified.

> *The Congress shall have Power to declare the Punishment of Treason, but no Attainder of Treason shall work Corruption of Blood, or Forfeiture except during the Life of the Person attainted.*

Congress alone can determine the punishment for Treason, but specific restrictions are put in place.

The Corruption of Blood is to claim that a family relation should be punished in place of, or in addition to, the guilty party. In many nations, the use of family members to pressure people to confess is common. Our founders wisely chose to eliminate these options, for they lent themselves to abuse.

They also limited punishments to within a persons life. This again limits the effective punishments, as anything forfeited for Treason cannot be taken after the traitor has passed on. . Land taken, stocks seized, whatever is determined as punishment begins, and ends, with the person themselves. If they pass on before they are punished, there is to be no punitive application against the traitors heirs.

Article. IV.

Section. 1.

Full Faith and Credit shall be given in each State to the public Acts, Records, and judicial Proceedings of every other State. And the Congress may by general Laws prescribe the Manner in which such Acts, Records and Proceedings shall be proved, and the Effect thereof.

A nation which ignores its own responsibilities is a nation not long for this world. To ensure this, we have the Full Faith and Credit clause, which is an agreement that each state will accept the legal decisions from other states. A person who is convicted of murder in one state cannot live in another to avoid punishment. A person who is divorced in one state cannot remain married to their former spouse in another. There is a limit to this, of course, but all legal decisions, contracts, and records from one state are to be accepted in all.

This section is one often forgotten in the debates over the years. Time and again the Supreme Court has had to reassert that this section is to be adhered to. But states continue to ignore the implications. For example, Loving vs Virginia, the state of Virginia tried to claim that it did not have to recognize the marriage of the Lovings because the state did not accept interracial marriage. But according to this clause, Virginia, all states in fact, have to accept that the Lovings, all interracial marriages, are to have their marriage licenses, a legal document, accepted. Same with birth certificates, divorce settlements, and so forth. Now, this section allows the federal government to have some restrictions, such as limiting marriage to between two people, but anything over and above that the states have to accept each others records.

Section. 2.

The Citizens of each State shall be entitled to all Privileges and Immunities of Citizens in the several States.

Beyond accepting the records of each other state, our Constitution requires honoring the privilege and immunity enjoyed by citizens of the other states as well. This provision means, for instance, that if you are wed in one state, all other states must accept the rights you enjoy as a person wed to another in the other states. Combine this seemingly small and insignificant provision with the Full Faith and Credit clause above, and we find a very powerful combination of powers given to the Federal government, and limiting the states in a significant manner.

But, further, it does not limit us to merely while occupying each state, but that every citizen gains the privileges and immunities found in every state, as a whole, regardless of which state they currently occupy. This is a problem for state legislatures, which currently try and exploit differences in law. Properly, they need to honor the privileges and immunities granted amongst each other.

The simplest solution would be to realize that even attempting to do this is impossible. The only rational solution is that privilege, and immunity, is a federal, not state, level function of government. States do not decide upon rights, they decide upon local ordinance, criminal code, taxation within their borders. But as part of the United States, the various states have declared that they are united in what a citizen represents. It is time we honor this idea, and eliminate the preposterous notion of per-state rights.

A Person charged in any State with Treason, Felony, or other Crime, who shall flee from Justice, and be found in another State, shall on Demand of the executive Authority of the State from which he fled, be delivered up, to be removed to the State having Jurisdiction of the Crime.

The idea of fleeing one territory to escape justice is as old as the very idea of laws themselves. But, within our Constitution, this idea is thrown out. Instead, upon the demand of a State's executive, another state shall deliver up one accused of a crime.

However, that little section is too often ignored. Instead of the executive issuing the demand, courts of even the police directly issue these requests. There is a reasoning why this is put upon the executive of the state, rather than the bureaucracy which is being ignored here. It needs to be important enough to warrant the attention of the executive. It is critical to maintain this, rather than merely waving it away as some trivial passage to be used or ignored at their leisure.

The concern over abuse of the fleeing statute of the Constitution is why we have this oversight over criminal proceedings. Having the executive authority of the state issuing such demands, rather than a court system directly, gives much needed oversight on a system which is otherwise easy to abuse.

No Person held to Service or Labour in one State, under the Laws thereof, escaping into another, shall, in Consequence of any Law or Regulation therein, be discharged from such Service or Labour, but shall be delivered up on Claim of the Party to whom such Service or Labour may be due.

This is an interesting provision. Those who are obliged to service may not vacate that service through fleeing to another. This is to prevent tricks such as failing to appear at a legislative session for a state by that states legislature by hiding in another. We had an issue some years back where a sizable number of state legislators from Texas went to Oklahoma in order to prevent legislation from passing. This section of the US Constitution strictly forbids such antics.

This is yet another provision of our Constitution which is ignored, despite the critical role it serves. When one is bound for service, they must stay to complete said service. Failure to do so then makes the group liable for retrieval through the same executive function as criminal cases. Yes, we can all admire these kinds of antics when it is "our side" doing them, but they undermine the system itself, and that will not do. They need to find another solution, and not some legislative shenanigans.

Section. 3.

New States may be admitted by the Congress into this Union; but no new State shall be formed or erected within the Jurisdiction of any other State; nor any State be formed by the Junction of two or more States, or Parts of States, without the Consent of the Legislatures of the States concerned as well as of the Congress.

From the beginning, the United States viewed itself as expansive. They planned for growth from day one. But it was not to be an easy process. As we see here, adding a new state is relatively simple, but forming a new state out of another is quite tricky.

There was a concern in our earliest stages that a multitude of states would gang up on a larger, in order to split it into parts. This would, they theorized, reduce their power or influence in Congress. So, to split a state, there had to be a more elaborate system than to merely accept one.

> *The Congress shall have Power to dispose of and make all needful Rules and Regulations respecting the Territory or other Property belonging to the United States; and nothing in this Constitution shall be so construed as to Prejudice any Claims of the United States, or of any particular State.*

Again, we find that Congress has final arbitration over the territory controlled by the United States.

And again, the issue we have is that these territories were envisioned as unpopulated areas of control, not areas such as Washington D.C., with populations larger than many states.

Section. 4.

> *The United States shall guarantee to every State in this Union a Republican Form of Government, and shall protect each of them against Invasion; and on Application of the Legislature, or of the Executive (when the Legislature cannot be convened), against domestic Violence.*

A concern we must always keep in mind is that the states are not identical to the federal government. Each state has their own legislative structure, their own executive, their own laws, and so forth. While the federal trumps all, state, and local, governments are needed. While the Constitution leaves the local administration up in the air, the Constitution does require an elected government for the state level of control.

The concern is over a non-representative government. Just as with federal representation no longer reflecting the People, we witness state governments which are no longer representing those who, nominally, they are there to serve. Be it from a prison-industrial complex, legalized bribery or party bosses, the states have in many cases eroded into structures by which the moneyed elite can run roughshod over the People.

When Michigan enacted laws allowing the governor to overrule local elections, and appoint an unelected manager for cities and towns, it foretold the future for our nation. Local municipals handle elections, through operation of polling places in many cases. By having someone stripping local electoral power, the legitimacy of elections can and should be called into question.

When the system becomes so tilted that honest debate is impossible, where disenfranchisement becomes routine, the system is perverted beyond what is allowed in this section, by any interpretation. It is not just a one-time deal here, after all. It is a continuing, living system, which means when a state fails to live up to the promise of a representative Republic, the federal government has the authority to step in.

In return, the states gain protection from the federal government. This is not some hollow gesture, but is tied closely to the Militia, as outlined first in Article 1, Section 8, but further elaborated in the 2nd Amendment below. It even states that the federal will be used to enforce the Legislative passed measures, which is precisely why the Militia was mentioned beforehand.

Without this provision, there would be no mechanism by which laws could be enforced in any sane or reasonable construct. While we have interpreted this section so oddly, some may even say ignored it utterly, it is a critical section to say the least.

As a result, this passage means "Unless your state represents the people within, it shall not have its laws enforced." The state must have legitimacy, it must have voter mandates. It must be representative of the People within it. This means measures deigned to remove voting rights would in turn render the state unable to meet its obligation as a constituent Republic, and could find itself under martial law.

Re-read the words again, The United States shall *Guarantee* a Republican form of Government. Not just states pledging that they will have one, but a solemn guarantee from the Federal government that a representative based republican government shall be enacted in each state, or else. And it is the Federal government, not the states, which is the final arbiter of this, as written here plain to see.

Article. V.

The Congress, whenever two thirds of both Houses shall deem it necessary, shall propose Amendments to this Constitution, or, on the Application of the Legislatures of two thirds of the several States, shall call a Convention for proposing Amendments, which, in either Case, shall be valid to all Intents and Purposes, as Part of this Constitution, when ratified by the Legislatures of three fourths of the several States, or by Conventions in three fourths thereof, as the one or the other Mode of Ratification may be proposed by the Congress; Provided that no Amendment which may be made prior to the Year One thousand eight hundred and eight shall in any Manner affect the first and fourth Clauses in the Ninth Section of the first Article; and that no State, without its Consent, shall be deprived of its equal Suffrage in the Senate.

Here is how the US Constitution is to be amended. This outlines not one, but two different modes to propose, and pass, an amendment, while also leaving open an option for Congress to add yet more avenues to the process.

To date, no Constitutional Convention for proposing Amendments has been held. The bar for an Amendment is high, regardless, with ¾ of the states needing to sign off on any new Amendment along with 2/3 of Congress. Note what is obvious by its absence here is that no Presidential signature, nor judicial oversight is given for this process. This is strictly between the states and federal government.

There is even one more option, than just the state's legislature. Namely, an in-state convention. The terms and conditions of this are not defined, but that it exists tells us that there exists options for the future.

As well, they reiterated that a states representation within the Senate is not to be meddled with. Beyond that however, it is wide open.

And it is this "other Mode of Ratification" which opens an interesting window here, a crack through which we could introduce a new option, the citizen proposal.

Several states allow for citizens to draft amendments. This can be good, it can be bad. But it can be a handy tool for us here.

Let us say that we put forth a new "Mode of Ratification," one which retains the state and federal legislatures and percentages nominally, but adds the ability for citizens to directly propose ideas to be weighed on. Set rules by which these ideas may be presented to the people, and let the people speak.

We do not need an Amendment to do so, nor our legislators directly. Further, this Citizens Initiative action could allow for a direct electoral overruling of a state legislature. The same percentage is still in place, so a ¾ majority of the states would need to support the motion. A tall hill, but not an impossible one.

Same system, but with an added layer clearly noted, a direct democratic layer. While direct democracy is not always the wisest action, if the electorate feels so strongly about an issue that they would vote to over-rule their elected officials, then there is a disconnect which needs to be addressed regardless.

Article. VI.

All Debts contracted and Engagements entered into, before the Adoption of this Constitution, shall be as valid against the United States under this Constitution, as under the Confederation.

While now obsolete, these debts having been paid off centuries ago, this provision does give a guide for the handling of our debts. They are not to be skipped out on, and always to be handled.

With the regular threats to default on our debts, our congress needs a reminder that within the Constitution itself this section exists. All debts and engagements shall be valid.

This Constitution, and the Laws of the United States which shall be made in Pursuance thereof; and all Treaties made, or which shall be made, under the Authority of the United States, shall be the supreme Law of the Land; and the Judges in every State shall be bound thereby, any Thing in the Constitution or Laws of any State to the Contrary notwithstanding.

The states, and by extension, the people within them, are bound to the Constitution. But in so doing, the Constitution is also bound to them, and they are bound to each other.

This is the core of the social compact, the unspoken contract between us all as citizens of the United States. We count on each other to follow the laws and order we create together. And when these laws are unjust, we must work together to correct them.

The Senators and Representatives before mentioned, and the Members of the several State Legislatures, and all executive and judicial Officers, both of the United States and of the several States, shall be bound by Oath or Affirmation, to support this Constitution; but no religious Test shall ever be required as a Qualification to any Office or public Trust under the United States.

As before, an oath, or pledge, is taken as seriously as any other compact. To take office, they must swear to uphold the Constitution, the laws, and society itself.

But here, we find a new provision, a prohibition against religious based tests or oaths. With these simple words, "No Religious Test shall ever be required as a Qualification to any Office or public Trust under the United States," we find not a preference, not a dislike, but a complete and total ban upon religious metrics for service. Not just to take an office, but for any form of public trust.

This is often times forgotten in the hyper-religious attitudes carried by some today. Our Constitution leaves no room for interpretation here – religious tests are strictly forbidden. That our founders left no wiggle room should tell us all how important such a provision was to them. With few words, they gave a very profound lesson for us all.

First and foremost, our duty is not to our gods, but to each other. For if we cannot care for ourselves, how can we fulfill whatever religious obligations we may have?

Article. VII.

The Ratification of the Conventions of nine States, shall be sufficient for the Establishment of this Constitution between the States so ratifying the Same.

The Word, "the," being interlined between the seventh and eighth Lines of the first Page, The Word "Thirty" being partly written on an Erazure in the fifteenth Line of the first Page, The Words "is tried" being interlined between the thirty second and thirty third Lines of the first Page and the Word "the" being interlined between the forty third and forty fourth Lines of the second Page.

Attest William Jackson Secretary

done in Convention by the Unanimous Consent of the States present the Seventeenth Day of September in the Year of our Lord one thousand seven hundred and Eighty seven and of the Independance of the United States of America the Twelfth In witness whereof We have hereunto subscribed our Names,

G°. Washington Presidt and deputy from Virginia **New York** Alexander Hamilton	**South Carolina** J. Rutledge Charles Cotesworth Pinckney Charles Pinckney Pierce Butler
Delaware Geo: Read Gunning Bedford jun John Dickinson Richard Bassett Jaco: Broom	**Georgia** William Few Abr Baldwin **New Hampshire** John Langdon Nicholas Gilman
Maryland James McHenry Dan of St Thos. Jenifer Danl. Carroll	**New Jersey** Wil: Livingston David Brearley Wm. Paterson Jona: Dayton
Virginia John Blair James Madison Jr.	**Massachusetts** Nathaniel Gorham Rufus King
Pensylvania B Franklin Thomas Mifflin Robt. Morris Geo. Clymer Thos. FitzSimons Jared Ingersoll James Wilson Gouv Morris	**Connecticut** Wm. Saml. Johnson Roger Sherman **North Carolina** Wm. Blount Richd. Dobbs Spaight Hu Williamson

And with the signatures attached, our Constitution was turned from mere idea into the grand experiment. These men would have no idea the turmoil, or ideas, which would cross our nations path. They took a leap of faith, and put their trust in not only each other, but in the People themselves.

And if they can do that, so too can the rest of us.

Amendment I

Congress shall make no law respecting an establishment of religion, or prohibiting the free exercise thereof; or abridging the freedom of speech, or of the press; or the right of the people peaceably to assemble, and to petition the Government for a redress of grievances.

Now, here we often times hear said that the United States has freedom of religion. But, reading here, there is no such freedom granted nor expressed. Instead what we have is a prohibition, that the government cannot pass a law to even respect the establishment of religion, or of prohibiting the exercise of the religion. This is not a freedom of religion itself, but a freedom of individual rights. It is a prohibition of the government from abridging an individuals right to religious practice, but there is no such prohibition on the religious organizations aside from the establishment of religion. Once the religion is established, the government can give oversight as needed, so long as it is not giving preferential status to one over the other (due to the earlier provision preventing a religious affirmation or oath).

As such, this is in effect not a freedom of religion, but a clear prohibition of official recognition of religion on a governmental level. It is the other half of what Thomas Jefferson called the "Wall of Separation between Church and State." It leaves individuals free to exercise their own faiths, but gives no formal support nor promise that the government will leave church organizations free from regulation.

This fits in with much of how our founders understood religions at that time. Churches were small, organization loose, and faith a highly personal item. That is how they need to stay, personal, and not the mega-enterprises we find today. These super-churches threaten the very idea of the United States with their claims of divine right and push for a theocratic government. As such, they need to be broken up, like trusts of old, and faith itself restored to the people.

The Freedom of Speech is one which is widely interpreted, and widely abused. The claim is such that this means people are free to express themselves however they wish, without fear of consequence. That is not what is written however. Instead of it being an unlimited right for people to misbehave, instead the only thing on restriction is that it will not be abridged – that is, people will not be deprived of their freedom to speak. There is nowhere in there which gives people the freedom from consequence. If someone were to yell fire in a theatre, they would be liable for the damage caused.

This is something long forgotten in many court cases as of late, that the freedom to speak is not a freedom of consequence. We have court decisions which list money as speech, enabling those with more cash to out-speak those without. This brings a weight of consequence which needs to be addressed. The freedom of speech is an individual right, as such all people must be granted equal access to speak. We cannot let one person out-speak another, else we remove the viability of this right. If we do allow so, it becomes not a freedom of speech, but a freedom to shout.

If our public discourse becomes no more than shouting, it is no longer a freedom at all, but a distraction. And that is not acceptable in any society. Freedom of Speech when combined with equal access and with the inherent acceptance of responsibility is a powerful tool for the people to have their voices heard. That is why this push by the would-be oligarchy to suppress this. While they claim to be lobbying for freedom of speech, the result of their actions, the consequence, is the direct harm for the people to speak their minds and have their voices heard. That is what they aim to destroy, through shouting—suppression of unwanted speech through monetary strangulation, ensuring their Oligarchy and its message is the only one accepted.

As with the freedom to swing ones arm, that freedom ends when it impacts someone else. Not all positions will be popular ones, nor will every person listen, but the freedom to speech must enable that those who would listen are able to. Also, it must allow for those who do not wish to listen, also be able to. A neo-Nazi rally in front of a Synagogue would render itself impossible to not be heard, even if one wished.

This freedom therefore comes at a cost, that the audience is the one which determines how free to speak one is, not those speaking. A newsletter offered upon request is fully allowed, no matter how vile the content. A billboard showing dismembered baby parts along a freeway is not allowed, no matter how much freedom the speaker desires.

This concept, of individual freedom of speech being as much a part of the listener as the speaker, has been lost in modern debates.

For the press, that is the independent media of journalism, similarly it was not to be curtailed. This did not mean that one could post a series of lies and claim journalistic freedom, for once again we do not have the freedom from consequence. False reporting can, and would, be strictly punished. Honesty and accuracy in reporting is critical, one of the reasons why our founders called the press the fourth branch of government. Their role is to educate, to inform, and not to bias. And it must be available to the audience, when the audience asks, not pushed upon them in some manner or another.

This does not mean they cannot have an opinion. Opinion-Editorials are older than even this country, and editors do need the freedom to express opinions, when and only clearly positioned as opinions. It must be divested however from the press itself, not intermingled so as to make it difficult to differentiate between news and gossip. While the scandal press is a popular medium in Britain, in the United States its reputation has never been strong, and for good reason. It has no place in popular society, for the sensationalism used often times discredits the real news which often times does appear within.

Instead it is relegated, wisely, to a section clearly marked for such press, for the fringe, the innuendo and rumor – the Tabloid.

Today we have a lot of blending between these however. We have news channels which are truly nothing but tabloids, yet are presented as honest newscasting. This needs to end, and those who freely mix opinion with journalism marked accordingly. This is not a restriction of press, but an enforcement of consequence. The liberal mixing of opinion with journalism undermines the entire press apparatus, and in turn hurts the people as they seek to educate themselves on the important issues of the day. That means holding press accountable. If an agency wishes to be called a member of the press, they must be held to a higher standard. Otherwise, they descend below the radar and can be safely ignored.

One area which has been contentious as of late has been the right to assemble peacefully. As written, that right cannot be abridged, but as with other rights here, it can bring consequence. If gathered in the middle of the street without prior clearance, an assembled group might find themselves injured by traffic. If gathered on a train track, well, the picture is not pretty. Gather a huge crowd in a small, enclosed space, and someone starts a fire, you get the idea.

To handle this, we created a permitting system. We agreed, as a society, to create a system by which people who were to gather notified the location ahead of time. This way the necessary government body could review, and make sure no obvious problems could arise. This has, however, been abused in many cases, such as the designation of "Free Speech Zones" miles from an event to protest. While it fits the letter of the Constitution, it is a clear violation of the spirit when it is applied in a hap-hazard manner.

Where are these "Free Speech Zones" for OB/GYN clinic protests? For those who protest against business practices? We cannot grant politicians or public institutions safe zones and eliminate them for the People at large. So, if we are to have "Free Speech Zones" they must be equally applicable. If we are to have them for politicians, then they must exist for other, non-public entities as well. A permit system as we have already can be adapted for such purpose. It needs to be applied equally between both private and public entities. Either both can have the insulation, or neither can.

When it comes to petitioning the government for the redress of grievances, the United States is in a very sad state. Going back to the notion of money being speech, it also is access. Today, it is very difficult, if not impossible, for the average citizen to effectively petition the government to redress anything. Those who come calling with campaign contributions, or what throughout history would be called bribes, are always given preferential treatment to those who come with a mere collection of signatures.

All too often, petitioning the government gives the impression that it is little more than a waste of time. The failure of our elected officials to weigh in on issues which we feel are important then turns off public participation in the system. After all, do you feel valued when you are all but ignored? By devaluing those with issues from the people, by granting value to those with issues fueled by wealth, disillusionment over the system is inevitable.

As Thomas Paine so described, such freedom is not isolated, but interdependent upon each and every one of us. When we allow one person to have more access to freedom than another, they dominate the discourse. And in turn, they eliminate the opportunity for each and every one of us. Freedom in isolation is not freedom at all, but solitude. Freedom can only exist in community, in society.

Amendment II

A well regulated Militia, being necessary to the security of a free State, the right of the people to keep and bear Arms, shall not be infringed.

No amendment has been so diversely interpreted, and so incorrectly interpreted, as this one. There are whole lobbying groups dedicated to what they claim is the preservation of this amendment which simultaneously leave off half of it in order to present their interpretation.

On one side, you have a lobby which claims that this is on gun ownership, that the people have the right to own and use any and all weapons they so wish. They call this a fundamental right, and many even will go so far as to claim that this right exists in order to overthrow the dutifully elected government itself. This is preposterous on the face of it. A right to overthrow a government through arbitrary means cannot exist within the document which frameworks that same government.

On the other, you have a lobby which argues that this is on the use of military capability, that the government cannot disarm the militia, or national guard. The claim here is that the purpose of this amendment was to keep a level of state control over our national defense, and that this amendment is not over gun ownership at all.

Both of these arguments have some level of correctness, but are fundamentally wrong. Nowhere in any of this amendment is there any statement of ownership, by either people or the military. It is about the right of action, and participation, not in the right of property.

You will find those who will claim that the first portion, "A well regulated militia, being necessary for a free state," is a qualifying statement, framing the scope and purpose of the amendment. However, such statements are not used anywhere else in the US Constitution. Why would it be used here of all places? It clearly cannot be the case, so this section must be something else.

Eliminating these earlier interpretations, what we find is that the subject of this amendment is not people, nor rights, but the Militia itself. Earlier, we established that the militia is to be regulated, which is reaffirmed here. But, at the same time, we have established that the militia's first role is for law enforcement, not for military service. This makes the next piece more important.

We find an Adjective Clause, "being necessary for a free state," immediately following the subject of Militia. This is a goal, a mission statement as it were, why this measure is needed. We find this several other times in the US Constitution, including in the 1st Amendment – a clarification as to why we have key provisions and portions included. This is also very important, and the importance of it will become clear in a moment.

The last portion is the only section which many appear to care anything for, even as it does not make grammatical sense. As a sentence "the right of the people to keep and bear Arms, shall not be infringed." tells us very little, and is so broad as to effectively meaningless. Which tells us that this cannot be viewed independently, and must be part of the earlier sentence. The right of the people is the object of the sentence, that which is being modified or upheld, since keep and bear arms is a verb in this case.

Since we have already established that the Militia is to serve as the primary police force, to enforce the law, what we have here is the mechanism by which we prevent this police force from becoming a power unto itself – the People have the right to keep and bear arms as part of the Militia – to be part of the Militia. This amendment is over the ability to join our law enforcement and last line of national defense, not guns at all.

Every person has the right to be part of our collective protection system. The right to join in our militia, for enforcing our laws, for defending against insurrection and invasion, shall not be infringed. Every person who is of age has the right to keep and bear arms within the well-regulated, government managed militias.

This addresses a real problem we have today, that the police lack the accountability needed for legitimacy. As it stands, the police are kept independent of the people which they are to serve. This can result in the Police becoming a power unto themselves, and as a result are difficult to regulate and manage.

This amendment addresses that problem, a problem the founding fathers recognized too well – hereditary law enforcement. They had just fought a war against a nation which had whole families who inherited the role of sheriff, knight, or other law enforcement title. They saw the corruption which was inherent in such a system, and knew that the only way to prevent that was to make it impossible to exclude others from service.

By excluding the people, by being independent of the people, our police becomes insular, self-serving – they exist for the sake of existing. Police departments began as a way to address a problem of law enforcement during time of conflict. Today, they exist in order to validate their own existence. As we have witnessed these past few years, it is difficult to prosecute an officer for breaking the law.

The ability to hold our law enforcement accountable is compromised from the permanent nature of our police force. Prosecutors are reluctant to press charges against an officer who helped them in another case earlier, who may help them in cases in the future. Police departments do not self-regulate due to the us-vs-them mentality which an independent agency fosters over time. Cities cannot regulate else face election issues as candidates are listed as "soft on crime" if they hold departments accountable for their abuses. It is a self-perpetuating system, one which needs to be torn down.

By establishing that the militia is to handle the basic role of law enforcement, this changes that nature, but only if the militia remains of the People. The 2nd Amendment now locks this in, the formation of an accountable defense force. The people who are to be served also must be allowed to serve. Any person may join our law enforcement entity, our militia, to keep and bear arms for the enforcement of our laws as passed by the federal, state and local governments.

However, this opens up an avenue for both firearms regulation, while also securing gun ownership rights. As the People can join the militia, that is, the law enforcement organization, police, then the People would need access to the same form of firearms which we authorize law enforcement to use. The courts, through decisions as *D.C. vs Heller* have said that access needs to be fair, equitable, and not tied to military service. But they have also has said that states, cities and towns have a vested interest in regulating firearm ownership and access, so they need an avenue for doing so in a non-infringing manner.

Remembering the Militia's primary role as our law enforcement, and giving our various levels of government the authority to set the maximum level of firepower that law enforcement is given, it becomes clear that an equal-application here is precisely the form the founding fathers intended. A mob better armed than those who need to control it can riot without end. A police force better armed than the citizens can force its will and abuse the rights of the People. By making them parity, equal, with the ability to migrate from one to the other, we make a system which can reach balance, equality, and genuine fairness.

The founders understood that the militia needed to be civilians, not an elite group, inherited through families or private institutions such as trade associations. That any person who wished to serve, may serve, and is trained to serve by the state in which they live. That the right to keep and bear arms for the enforcement of our laws, and the defense of our nation, shall not be infringed.

Those who argue for personal weapons at the expense of public safety, for unfettered ownership without any restrictions, or to defend themselves from the government which they themselves are a part of as citizens of the United States are properly looking for tyranny. By denying this simple, and specific requirement that our defensive force be of civilians, and not gentried nobility, the end result of any such mass unrestricted firearm ownership policy is nothing but anarchy and chaos.

Amendment III

No Soldier shall, in time of peace be quartered in any house, without the consent of the Owner, nor in time of war, but in a manner to be prescribed by law.

Continuing the idea of granting a preference for the Civilian over the Military we saw earlier in the Constitution proper and in the 2nd Amendment, the 3rd Amendment puts even further restrictions upon the military force – not the Militia, which is made out of the people itself. Initial review is simple, that soldiers are not to be housed in civilian housing without permission.

There are those however who would see this as a far broader measure, that it would prevent any government oversight over private property. While the argument can be made, that is an incredible stretch.

A much simpler interpretation is that this amendment is there to protect a modicum of privacy. Indeed, we can find court cases, such as in *Griswold v Connecticut* (1965), where it was declared just that. The logic of these case examples is that with a soldier in the household, one would not have privacy. Much like the 2nd Amendment above, we face indirect rights, ones which are needed to make the defined rights work.

If there were no right to privacy, then the quartering would be unimportant, a mere inconvenience – no need for an amendment at all. But with it, this amendment makes the most sense. The People have the right to privacy within the confines of their own home, without an agent of the government intruding without permission.

By reinforcing the interpretation, it can be found that espionage programs, such as NSA domestic spying, is a clear violation of the 3rd Amendment. It was there to give us privacy, but here is a government agency, active soldiers in the war against terrorism, residing virtually within our homes.

We already have an issue of a militarized police overstepping their boundaries, quartering themselves in peoples homes for some task or mission. History demonstrates that such programs over time will eventually become nothing more than a way to keep the People in line for the oligarchs.

Recall the billet receipts from 16th century England. The soldiers were, nominally, to pay for the housing and any goods taken, but the reality is that the payments were often times worthless. And pray that the soldier was an honorable one, lest they exact a heavier price from the household's occupants.

In the modern, electronic espionage world we face, the violations we face we may never even know of. Body imaging scanners, camera controlling spyware, the avenues by which we can each be virtually violated grow by the day. The most intimate of moments, to be broadcast in secret, and shared among anonymous strangers without you ever being aware. The scenario is far more horrifying than anything our founding fathers could have foreseen.

While these soldiers are not flesh and blood, they are as real as those we see on the battlefield. They are software, malicious applications, computer viruses, and a wide variety of electronic surveillance equipment. The use of these without oversight is clearly unconstitutional under this interpretation.

Keeping this in mind, the importance of the amendment so often forgotten is quite significant. One should note that as a limitation of behavior for the soldier, it carries with it a far heavier burden. As such, this would apply wherever our soldiers are found.

The 3rd Amendment is a very powerful, if understated piece of the Constitution, protecting far more than what we found in the first two. A persons right to privacy is a powerful thing, an important thing, something so precious because once it is violated, it can never be regained.

Amendment IV

The right of the people to be secure in their persons, houses, papers, and effects, against unreasonable searches and seizures, shall not be violated, and no Warrants shall issue, but upon probable cause, supported by Oath or affirmation, and particularly describing the place to be searched, and the persons or things to be seized.

An issue common in the interpretations present in our system today is the heavy focus on this area as an individual right. This is a flaw in thinking, one which cripples our legal system from top to bottom.

As presented, this is not individual, but collective in design. The people have the right to be secure. Not a person, but the people as a whole. Without the greater community, an individual is lost among the chatter, their rights unable to be supported. No two cases are the same, no two people identical, which means as an individual only expression, it would be routine to violate, or ignore, this right.

We can witness this already in the near routine search and seizures on city streets. Stop and Frisk policies, profiling, the avenues of unconstitutional acts is compounded with the ease by which information gathering can be had.

As witnessed in the 3rd Amendment, we have a right to privacy. Here is the avenue by which the government, through its agents, may intrude on that privacy when needed. It is, like all other such intrusions, to be overseen by the court system, through warrants. And, by seeking warrants, the officers of government are putting their own necks on the line.

In all of this, we find checks and balances. Here, the officer requesting the warrant must be specific with the request, and must declare under Oath that it is accurate. Enough of these oaths fail to live up, the court is supposed to stop accepting the officer's oath, and stop issuing warrants. In other words, hold the officer accountable.

An officer who runs off to grab every warrant imagined, would miss so many that they would find themselves unable to secure any. That is how a working system would handle it. Yes, any officer will have an incorrect assumption, but that is why the job is to be absolutely certain first. A single error, it happens. Dozens, one right after the other, it is now negligence.

And with the switch of roles, for police officers now to be no longer the front line in law enforcement, this would in turn reduce the demand for such warrants in the first place. If an issue grew to the point that an officer would need a warrant, it would have, in theory, already passed through the civilian Watch, the Militia.

Checks and balances.

But it goes further. It is not just a request, but a very specific request. Warrants are to be incredibly detailed, specifying who, where, and why it is needed. No asking for warrants for "every red haired person with an overbite in lower Manhattan." We need these requests to be very specific.

Which is where we are failing as a nation. Now we allow warrant-less wiretaps, group warrants (in clear violation of the prohibition against Bill of Attainders) and other measures in the fight for security. But the security they promise is little more than the false hope against what goes bump in the night.

Benjamin Franklin once said "They that can give up essential liberty to obtain a little temporary safety deserve neither liberty nor safety." He was judging the action, but in hindsight those which do wind up with neither. In trading our liberty for the promise of security in the wake of 9/11, rather than a more secure nation, we have become a more paranoid nation while trading away our freedoms for nothing more than a security blanket.

The requirement for these extreme programs was sold on the avenue of added security, but the reality is we experience just as many terrorist attacks now as we did before, if not more. Many of the ones we face now are home grown, lone wolf actions by those who have been fed a steady stream of paranoia and delusion.

Rather than a well balanced system protecting liberty, we now have a system feeding the very terrorist activities it was created to protect us from. By stripping away the collective rights of the People, we find those who feel powerless and lash out in anger, often times after it is too late.

Through the restoration of the Militia, the elimination of over-arching intelligence agency, and the focus of police officers and warrants to their core issue, it would also serve to help prevent such lone wolf activities to begin with. We must give people this sense of ownership, that they are indeed their brothers keeper, and that we are all in this grand experiment together.

Having stripped that, is it any wonder that more and more people turn to the most violent of acts in order to give themselves the illusion of control?

Amendment V

No person shall be held to answer for a capital, or otherwise infamous crime, unless on a presentment or indictment of a Grand Jury, except in cases arising in the land or naval forces, or in the Militia, when in actual service in time of War or public danger; nor shall any person be subject for the same offense to be twice put in jeopardy of life or limb; nor shall be compelled in any criminal case to be a witness against himself, nor be deprived of life, liberty, or property, without due process of law; nor shall private property be taken for public use, without just compensation.

The classic 5th Amendment. While often cited for self-incrimination, it is a far more diverse and nuanced system than that.

Its first clause is that of the Grand Jury. While today we most commonly associate Grand Juries with indictments, it is actually given two different, related options. The first is of the Presentment, and the second is the Indictment.

A Presentment is, quite literally, to formally present to the court. In reality, it is a Grand Jury deciding on what a person is to be charged with. This is rarely done, for often times those on the Grand Jury do not know nor understand the nuances of law, so may decide on an inappropriate charge.

As a result, most Grand Juries are most often used not for Presentment, just Indictment.

But is this right? I say no, it is not.

Grand Juries are called on a regular basis by the courts. When this is done, they need to be given far more leeway than is often done today. This means taking the step of removing them from the Prosecutor, and making them more accountable to the judge oversight directly.

This will require giving them access to legal advise. For this advise, they will need access to non-party lawyers. A specialized field of law would develop as a result, one not focusing on plaintiff or defense, but of advisers. All too often, juries are not given guidance, or worse, they are guided by those with a stake in the outcome.

This approach would grant our courts the Inquisitorial capability we find in courts overseas, without adding in the potential for abuse found in some nations. Being able to inquire, investigate, and find facts independent of cases, to develop and bring cases to the courts, ties in with the changes in our law enforcement discussed earlier.

The need for a better solution for accusations is clear, based on the failure of our court system to address the true ills of our society. At the same time, we cannot leave this only within the hands of the police and lawyers. The People need to be there, to give us both oversight and guidance of the process.

It does however specify that this system is not for use with the military, or on the Militia when pressed into service for time of war. This specificity is forgotten, with the military and police both claiming exemption when not serving in combat.

The military tribunal system needs to be reserved only for times of war. The current use of it for any and all purposes is not adequate, nor is it suitable for the role in which we put our military men and women. We have people serving today who violated military regulations, but not the law. This kind of second justice system for those who dedicate their lives to our nation can never be just, nor fair. Fair and Equal does not exist, as we all know.

Risking double jeopardy, the charging of the same person for a crime twice, is well established. However, the Constitution is not so narrow as to claim that only a single person can serve double jeopardy. It says "any person" may not be subject. Which means, if you charge someone with a crime, nobody else can be charged with the same offense, as it reads.

This would make it far more important to be certain of the accusation before bringing charges. This dovetails nicely with the earlier provisions, preventing widespread open-ended warrants. It means that prosecution must be narrow, focused, and absolute.

The most common citation of the 5th Amendment is that someone may not give evidence against themselves. This is limited to criminal cases. But this is, indirectly, abused almost every day. Our law enforcement has numerous avenues to get around this restriction, from coerced confessions given during interrogation to mandatory fingerprinting.

The 5th Amendment requires legal procedure to be adhered to – that is a Judge must be involved. This means information stated by a suspect cannot be used in a court of law, unless the suspect puts it before the court directly. A confession must be willingly given to the Judge or other appointed officer of the court, on the public record, not to a law enforcement officer. This should help prevent the most common avenue of civil complaints over law enforcement.

Fingerprints, DNA, etc, must require a court order. In theory, every request has a judge's signature on it, but many times we find corners being cut, proper policy ignored, in the push for conviction. But this failure to adhere to procedure only undermines the legitimacy of our legal system, and the law itself.

Amendment VI

In all criminal prosecutions, the accused shall enjoy the right to a speedy and public trial, by an impartial jury of the State and district wherein the crime shall have been committed, which district shall have been previously ascertained by law, and to be informed of the nature and cause of the accusation; to be confronted with the witnesses against him; to have compulsory process for obtaining witnesses in his favor, and to have the Assistance of Counsel for his defence.

As established in Article 3, the way in which courts operate is set forth. Already, trials must be in the states in which the crime had been committed. Also, they must have a Jury, long understood under British law to represent those who had the right to vote. But it left a few holes, and it is the 6th Amendment here which fills these holes.

Now, these trials are public, preventing secret trials which can never be verified or reviewed. The secret trial is a common habit of tinpot dictators worldwide, after all, even in the 18th century. And by being public, there exists the possibility for an external eye to review, and verify, the proceedings were fair, and honest.

The accused must be told exactly what it is they are being charged with. This may seem obvious, but a trial without even an accusation is not unheard of. These fishing expedition trials in effect try to find something with which a person can be charged, and are the hallmark again of a dictatorship.

Those accused have the right to face their accuser. This provision more than any other is abused in this day and age. How do you face a traffic camera, or a corporation? From a mere pragmatic standpoint, these two examples become untenable, and cannot truly reflect a just legal system. But, if they are the primary accuser, then it must be defended against, in open court.

But the defense is also given permission to present witnesses in their own defense. The denial of this has, sadly, become normal in our court system as of late. And note the key word, compulsory. Even if a witness does not wish to, they must testify for the defense if demanded.

And lastly, the right to Counsel. This part is the most laughable of our current legal system. The public defender is one of the most overworked in our entire process. While the prosecutor is given near unlimited budgets and access, the defense as appointed is starved. Only those with wealth can overcome this, paying for their own legal services.

What is overlooked here is that at no point in any of this system was the option for a private lawyer listed. All of these elements specify public, not private, counsel. Private lawyers will always be needed, of course, for the drafting of contracts, lawsuits, etc, but for criminal proceedings, the Constitution is clear that only Counsel appointed by the court is to be used.

This may of course be a private practice. It should be part of every lawyers license to have a set amount of hours for public defendants every quarter, say 25% of all work hours, of which a minimum of 15% need to be within the courtroom. By having it done in this manner, as a requirement to maintain their license to operate to do pro bono work assigned by the court, the public defense would gain the critical relief needed.

Since those accused of crime could not cherry pick their lawyer, or to pay for a specialized lawyer, it would prevent the common problem we find in today's court proceedings of there being one court system for the rich, and one for the poor.

A subtle shift, in one small area, and you produce a very different court system. Since it would be based on hours, and not cases, an assigned Counsel would not gain from accepting a plea deal. They would still be on the hook for owed hours. It then becomes in their best interest to give the best defense possible, something our current system is incapable of for 99% of accused.

Amendment VII

In Suits at common law, where the value in controversy shall exceed twenty dollars, the right of trial by jury shall be preserved, and no fact tried by a jury, shall be otherwise re-examined in any Court of the United States, than according to the rules of the common law.

Common law is a phrase referring to case law, the established decisions by the court. So, as cases are decided, they build upon each other, creating precedents. This is the provision most important to us for our task.

Our issue is that the precedents have been slanted to favor those with wealth and power. With so many of our court officers over the two centuries of the Constitution's existence being in the pocket of various interests, this will be also the challenge to overcome.

This is the Revolution itself.

To overcome precedents, one must establish precedents. This is how our existing structure came to be – one decision at a time. And that is how it can be undone as well. Each case must be built as part of a grander effort, just as the oligarchs have done.

There is a wish for rapid change, for overthrowing the established order. This can work, the concern then becomes the risk of throwing the baby out with the bathwater.

Amendment VIII

Excessive bail shall not be required, nor excessive fines imposed, nor cruel and unusual punishments inflicted.

This is an area in which gross abuse exists throughout our nation. Consider how many people are serving years for minor drug possession charges. Or how many of us have been fleeced by a bail system which enriches cities, counties and states. It is time to say enough is simply enough.

The first focus needs to be on bail itself. Bail as understood in the 18th century was a temporarily held payment, which would be returned when you appeared for trial. Today, "bail" refers more to the bail bondsman system, where you pay a third party who then does nothing but promise to be a bounty hunter if you fail to show up for court. This wild west form of bail encourages the setting of bail price at an ever higher dollar value, since the bond is for only a fraction of that. A privatized component of the justice system, one which rewards the oligarchs and penalizes the People.

To resolve this, the very term Excessive must be brought in line with the reality that one persons penalty is another persons excessive and can be safely ignored by a third person. The only real solution here is for a penalty system based not on an arbitrary value, but on the impact it would have on the persons life. In Finland, fines are handled as a percentage of income, based on the prior years tax returns. So, a person of modest means would pay significantly less than one who was well off. This is truly the only way in which excessive penalties can be avoided.

As well, we must eliminate the bail bond system entirely. No person should profit off of criminal activity. Yet that is what the bail bonding system does, enable people to gain their wealth strictly off the misfortune of others. This also then makes the impact of the bail felt, while also eliminating the temptation to use the system as a hidden tax by governments.

Fines must be handled in the same manner as bail, for otherwise one persons minor inconvenience is anothers excessive. A scale based on income would make fines hold weight for each person penalized in such a manner. Yet, by making it such a scale, it becomes difficult to use such a system as a hidden tax, as so many cities have been busted doing over the years.

Yet, where will these fines go? A fine is for restitution to those damaged by criminal activity. This means, any fines must go to the offended party. The state, county or municipal does not count as an offended party in any case, as established in the 11th Amendment. As a result, one cannot charge a fine for such behavior. This would ironically eliminate speeding tickets as a revenue system. This does not mean that speeding does not carry with it a penalty, but that the fee goes to the offended parties, the other drivers on the road. Imagine the psychological impact of getting a check once a month, with your portion of the "speeding payment." You speed, you forfeit your share.

This would bring a psychological component to the penalty. People would get a reminder month, after month, that if you speed, you will be forwarding your own money to other drivers, instead of getting it from offenders yourself.

For Cruel and Unusual Punishment, here is where our system is truly failing us.

Cruel punishments are those who cause direct harm to the offender. Cruelty is not tolerated, even against the guilty. But, our current system is designed to be Cruel, to dehumanize those who have violated our laws. And we act surprised how bad recidivism is within our judicial system? By being Cruel, we have created a system that is self perpetuating, where one in ten US citizens have seen the inside of the jail cell. This is an epidemic of imprisonment, and if that is not Cruel, then nothing is.

Unusual is to apply a penalty which is out of line with those given to others who have the same offense. This means the application of law must be uniform. But, with the wealthy of our nation having access to the best lawyers, to political favors, to donations to a judges campaign for office, the application of law is all but uniform. As a result, any penalty now can be labeled as Unusual.

The only solution is to pursue an equal judicial system, divorced from wealth or status. As discussed above, all counsel for defense must be court appointed, from the same pool, randomized, to eliminate the wealthiest criminals ability to lawyer shop. But in the penalty stage, it must be built around those found guilty, not out of some arbitrary penalty model we find today. And again, any penalty must not profit private interests. These new sweat shops of prison labor making clothing for sale must be eliminated. If a prisoner must labor, it must be for the public good, not for private wealth.

After all, it is the violation of the public trust which resulted in their incarceration to begin with.

Amendment IX

The enumeration in the Constitution, of certain rights, shall not be construed to deny or disparage others retained by the people.

The 9th Amendment is quite possibly the most important of those found within the Bill of Rights. It may seem small, and using the archaic language of the period, but what it states is simple – that the rights listed within the Constitution are not the whole of rights there are. This Amendment is what grants us the ability to explore and identify rights not expressly given, those which are found through interpretation or which are natural expansions to those given within. From Roe vs Wade to Loving vs Virginia, the 9th Amendment has served as the lynchpin for our civil liberties.

This does not mean that the rights come from the 9th Amendment, of course. What this means is that rights, as agreed by society, are to be respected, and supported regardless of the law. In Roe vs Wade, the decision was on body autonomy – that the same rights we give the dead to not be harvested for organs or tissue without permission given by either the person who died or their families also be given to a woman while she is still alive. In Loving vs Virginia it was that two people had the right to be wed – that the right does not change based on the color of their skin.

This relies heavily upon interpretation, so it can be confusing or muddled. And this Amendment over others is one which will mutate and change over time. It is a direct mirror of our society, the standards by which we hold dear.

Through the attempt to solidify our society into a rigid structure, social engineering through legal interpretation, it undermines the very principles of our nation. Such a rigid system cannot endure, it cannot survive, over the centuries, and would in time become little more than dictatorship with but lip service given to democratic principles.

Amendment X

The powers not delegated to the United States by the Constitution, nor prohibited by it to the States, are reserved to the States respectively, or to the people.

This Amendment discusses the division of power between the Federal Government, the States and the People themselves. The Constitution gives the Federal Government sweeping powers, but clearly defined ones. Beyond these defined powers, the powers are reserved for the States themselves, or barring them the People directly.

The Federal Government does not set traffic fines, the State or Local governments do that. Conversely, States cannot impose a tariff on good crossing their borders or mint their own currency. This division of power establishes the nature of government for our nation.

Of note, this also means that the Federal Government cannot force a State to perform its duties, nor could a State do so even if it wished. For example, in the immigration debate, several states attempted to motion for their own immigrant laws, but in so doing they violated the clear division line drafted here in the 10th Amendment.

This Amendment also means that when the Federal Government creates a program for the states to manage, it is up to the States to decide how they will manage it. A prime example of this is in Medicaid, where the Federal Government finances the program, sets the standards by which it operates, but the States set up and manage the system itself. What one find is true in one state's Medicaid program does not hold true nationwide.

Section after section of our government is handled in this manner, a ballet of duties with the Federal and State governments each in their own role upon the stage. What this means however is that each side can also force the other into very sticky situations.

Right now, we have a problem of exploitation in this country. We have companies which relocate from state to state in order to squeeze out the best deal from various governments, only to then relocate again whenever a better deal comes along. From tax incentives to free services, the end result is that our states wind up losing while the Oligarchs walk away with your tax dollars.

The 10th Amendment actually prohibits this however. While the states have power, they are not immutable, not limitless. The Federal Government is given the power for interstate commerce, and these businesses exploiting each state in turn clearly is interstate commerce. Once these companies expand to beyond the local sphere, it is the Federal government which is their overseer, not the state.

As such, per the 10th Amendment any attempt to exploit intra-state law differences or loopholes, or any differential in taxes, would need to be shut down. That means that any tax differential would need to be then added on at the Federal level, for instance.

Imagine the business which moves from tax-heavy California to tax-poor Texas, then finds their tax burdens followed them. It would discourage such state shopping quickly.

The simplest avenue here would be to make all state-level taxes deducted from the federal level so the overall tax level remains the same, across this nation. By doing so, now states which attempted to woo businesses through such incentives would find their own tax schemes imploding. We follow up with this on other levels so that every time a state tries to give some business a better deal, it hurts that business overall, and the gravy train our Oligarchs have counted on for centuries comes to an end.

AMENDMENT XI

Passed by Congress March 4, 1794. Ratified February 7, 1795.

The Judicial power of the United States shall not be construed to extend to any suit in law or equity, commenced or prosecuted against one of the United States by Citizens of another State, or by Citizens or Subjects of any Foreign State.

The 11th Amendment modified Article III, section 2, of the Constitution. In the wake of the *Chisholm v. Georgia* case in 1792, the court was faced with the issue that the state of Georgia had in effect declared that it could not be sued outside of its own state boundaries. In this case, the Supreme Court ruled that the federal courts would arbitrate cases whereby a citizen of one state could sue another state.

As a result, Congress passed the 11th Amendment, whereby such cases by US Citizens could not use the federal court system, but had to be handled within the states own courts. So, to sue the state of Georgia, one would need to file within Georgia.

However, this is not absolute, as *Fitzpatrick v. Bitzer* decided in 1976. In that case, it was decided that Congress can, thanks to the powers granted by the 14th Amendment, abrogate the states right to immunity. This means that states could not hide behind the 11th Amendment to avoid restitution, but retained the checks and balances which the US Constitution and the 11th Amendment were intended to reinforce. In addition, this did not apply to non-suit cases, nor did the protections of it apply to officers of the state nor state agencies. It was very narrow, and in this narrow interpretation it worked well at preventing overly broad litigation against the states.

Over the years however, this definition has been expanded, to the point that even a states own citizens cannot effectively petition the court over damages, from either an officer or agency, without the states own consent. We witness this used within the state of Michigan, where elected officials are ignored and unelected managers appointed by the governor to rule over fiefdoms without any avenue for accountability. This gives states incredible power, and eliminates oversight.

At this time, the only way to overcome the issue is, as mentioned above, for an act of Congress to enable it to proceed. By requiring this for every possibility of suit, this is a waste of the legislatures time, and as a result engineered to effectively mute civil rights violations by the states.

A return to the Marshall court narrow interpretation would also return accountability to our state legislatures. As it stands now, it is difficult, if not impossible to hold our states to the same standards we do for the rest of society.

AMENDMENT XII

Passed by Congress December 9, 1803. Ratified June 15, 1804.

Note*: A portion of Article II, section 1 of the Constitution was superseded by the 12th amendment.*

The Electors shall meet in their respective states and vote by ballot for President and Vice-President, one of whom, at least, shall not be an inhabitant of the same state with themselves; they shall name in their ballots the person voted for as President, and in distinct ballots the person voted for as Vice-President, and they shall make distinct lists of all persons voted for as President, and of all persons voted for as Vice-President, and of the number of votes for each, which lists they shall sign and certify, and transmit sealed to the seat of the government of the United States, directed to the President of the Senate; -- the President of the Senate shall, in the presence of the Senate and House of Representatives, open all the certificates and the votes shall then be counted; -- The person having the greatest number of votes for President, shall be the President, if such number be a majority of the whole number of Electors appointed; and if no person have such majority, then from the persons having the highest numbers not exceeding three on the list of those voted for as President, the House of Representatives shall choose immediately, by ballot, the President. But in choosing the President, the votes shall be taken by states, the representation from each state having one vote; a quorum for this purpose shall consist of a member or members from two-thirds of the states, and a majority of all the states shall be necessary to a choice. [And if the House of Representatives shall not choose a President whenever the right of choice shall devolve upon them, before the fourth day of March next following, then the Vice-President shall act as President, as in case of the death or other constitutional disability of the President. --]* The person having the greatest number of votes as

Vice-President, shall be the Vice-President, if such number be a majority of the whole number of Electors appointed, and if no person have a majority, then from the two highest numbers on the list, the Senate shall choose the Vice-President; a quorum for the purpose shall consist of two-thirds of the whole number of Senators, and a majority of the whole number shall be necessary to a choice. But no person constitutionally ineligible to the office of President shall be eligible to that of Vice-President of the United States.

After the election of 1800, it was clear that the original envisioned method for selecting the President was not going to work. The election became a near brawl fight between Thomas Jefferson and Aaron Burr. A new system was drafted, which rendered there to be independent ballots for both President and Vice President.

To resolve this, rather than the original "Winner becomes President, runner-up becomes Vice President" draft, we now find two votes, one for President and one for Vice President.

Yet, most states only cast one, with both on a single ticket. This is fine, if the Vice President is an executive subordinate of the President. However, our concept of moving the Vice President from a mere subordinate executive to the head of the Legislative upper body, makes the position far more important.

As this Amendment now makes the vote for Vice President now independent from President, we can take that division and make it available to the People in general as well. What traits we seek for a Head of State and those we seek for a Head of Government can be very different, after all. By dividing these roles, and giving the People the ability to pick these a la carte would serve us well.

When combined with later Amendments, this particular provision can become very important.

AMENDMENT XIII

Passed by Congress January 31, 1865. Ratified December 6, 1865.

Section 1.
Neither slavery nor involuntary servitude, except as a punishment for crime whereof the party shall have been duly convicted, shall exist within the United States, or any place subject to their jurisdiction.

The 13th Amendment altered a portion of Article IV, section 2, of the Constitution, and eliminated the idea of slavery and involuntary servitude. It came after a long and bloody civil war, one which cost hundreds of thousands of Americans their lives. The wounds it struck still are with us today. This amendment was created to wipe away the idea of one person owning another one, and the use of that person for uncompensated labor. Save, it did not.

It left in a provision which did maintain both as a punishment option for criminal offenses. The requirement for this was only if the person were "duly convicted." Duly is defined as *"in accordance with what is required or appropriate; following proper procedure or arrangement."* So, in other words, if the law prescribes as punishment your enslavement, so long as the law is followed, you can actually be enslaved.

And, as history demonstrates, that is precisely what has happened. As early as 1866, not only blacks, but poor of all walks, were being sold as slaves, convicted of a variety of crimes. A new crime entirely was introduced, "Vagrancy" to pad the new slave cells as part of what was called the "Convict Lease System." This is what former abolitionist Frederick Douglass described of the system.

> *(States) claim to be too poor to maintain state convicts within prison walls. Hence the convicts are leased out to work for railway contractors, mining companies and those who farm large plantations. These companies assume charge of the convicts, work them as cheap labor and pay the states a handsome revenue for their labor. Nine-tenths of these convicts are negroes.*

Which is the situation we have today. Prisons are now a system used for enslavement, to fill the pockets of the oligarchs who exploit those within. While the early programs such as the Convict Lease system were phased out, new ones were implemented, such as the Federal Prison Industries and a new private prison system.

Prison labor now is considered part of the Prison-Industrial Complex, a term used to cover the rapid expansion of prison populations, and the exploitation of the manpower within for cheap labor. Money generated feeds back in to the prison system, making an incentive for miscarriages of justice and undermining the legal system. We cannot consider this system as fulfilling the requirements set forth earlier in the 8th amendment, of prohibiting cruel or unusual punishment.

So, let us focus on the words a moment, "Duly" - in accordance with what is required. The provisions in the Bill of Rights, the 4th through 8th amendments, put forth a series of requirements for conviction. That would mean for such a punishment to be meted, not only would the person need to be indicted by a Grand Jury (5th Amendment), but convicted by a state-appointed Jury (6th amendment), with punishment then evaluated separately. There is no provision within the Constitution to allow for plea bargains or arbitration to be used for this provision. This amendment specifiably notes, the case must be duly convicted, and follow the full process from beginning to end. Otherwise this punishment, the insertion into indentured servitude or slavery, cannot be used.

This would chop off the prison industrial complex off at the knees. Most people who are in prisons have never stood before a jury of their peers. They have never been able to have suitable counsel. Their voice has been silenced due to a system which is focused on the barbaric concept that people are nothing more than disposable things, to either be used or discarded. Mandatory minimum sentencing is used as a club to force people to agree to bargains and reduce their sentence.

This is not the United States as established. It is not the ideal which we aim for. It is unacceptable for a civilized society to work in this way. The idea of secret trials, of not being given ones day in court before a jury of their peers, these are the actions of despots, not those of a free people. It is time we used the language of our Constitution, this language, to put an end to it.

If a criminal case bypasses any of these steps, the sentence is to be commuted, their indentured servitude ended. This would force the courts, and lawmakers, to reconsider their priorities. Laws designed to expand the criminal system would in turn hurt their ability to punish criminals. The courts would bog down, cases would drag out, and solutions which did not rely upon indentured servitude would need to be adopted.

And that is how our system is supposed to work. The 5th Amendment's requirement for due process, with clear steps, exists to prevent the kind of prison slavery we see today. Note how the 6th Amendment only refers to the trial as speedy, not the actual case. The process was never to be bypassed for expedience. If laws put down harsh punishments in order to shorten cases by bypassing the process, then the punishments themselves are to be mitigated. That is how the system is supposed to work, how our Constitution is framed to work.

Again, no amendment needed, just a change of view. By changing our interpretation, to meet the words presented and not what we've accepted in the name of expedience, it puts a barrier on overreach. A check and balance, precisely as our Constitution requires. It is the logical method to interpret this, and it grants us the protection to our collective freedoms sorely needed in this country.

Section 2.
Congress shall have power to enforce this article by appropriate legislation.

This piece of this and other Amendments may seem odd, but in the wake of the Civil War it was highly necessary. Some of what caused the war however was the assertion by some states that Congress could not enforce articles, it could not enforce the laws, if that state did not agree. Rather than re-fight a civil war which had already cost so many lives, Congress chose to include this simple statement, that they, and they alone, will have the power to enforce this article through legislation. And this would become a piece of amendments from here on out.

This was to prevent the various states from trying to circumvent the law, as they inevitably have done anyways. Congress over time failed to enforce this, letting our prison system become a de facto slave state.

This is easily corrected however, with a simple application of existing case law with basic interpretation. As found in *Lewis v. United States,* the courts found that cases which do not warrant such punishment do not require a jury trial. But, as a result it means that attempts to send people to prison, in an indentured role, does require a jury trial. Application is then found for our needs.

A simple step, one already supported but not realized in general. We operate how we do because it is how we always have, not because it is the right way. It is something we need to stop, together. Our prison system is no longer serving the public good, and the root cause is this interpretation, that people lose their rights upon incarceration.

By raising the bar for the process, we in turn force the courts to turn to alternative methods. Drug treatment, house arrest, therapy, the avenues become far more appealing for the courts. And that is the point. Our founders understood that the court system was not there for petty purpose, but for serious matter. By our disjointed criminal justice system operating as it is, it makes punishment take priority over justice, and the result is sentencing which no longer is related to the crime.

A murder conviction before the 13th Amendment was met with either capital punishment or a prison sentence of up to 10 years labor. Imagine that today, killing someone and only warranting 10 years. We have people sitting in prison from smoking a joint for far longer right now. The extending of sentences was based on the idea that labor was eliminated, but in our current system, it has been reintroduced, making the current prison system now a double punishment.

The idea of severe punishment for crimes is based on a long discredited idea, that crime and criminal behavior is an individual failing. This idea ignores the role in the greater society in creating the environment for this behavior. Poverty stricken areas are also crime ridden. A deregulated stock exchange also is crime ridden. The origin is the same, societies failure reflected upon the individual. We cannot expect the individual to bear this burden alone. Society must share this burden, else it will never fix the problems.

Consider the "Offender Lists" we find in various states. The idea began as a way to keep track of child abusers, but now we find such lists covering everything from nudists to someone who stole a pack of gum when they were 12. This is a continuing form of punishment, the deprivation of rights, without due process.

Criminal punishment is not to be perpetual, nor is it to be pervasive. It is to help turn the offender back into a productive member of society, or if that is not possible, to isolate them from society so as not to hurt others. The current criminal system does neither, and only perpetuates a system which does not help, but only hurts society.

By focusing on this narrower interpretation, that to be duly convicted the process must be completed and not bypassed or streamlined, it encourages the courts to leniency and mercy. And through so doing, it discourages the kind of behavior by our law enforcement and elected officials which have created the cycle of poverty which traps people across this nation.

As well, with this approach, it also discourages the behavior which enables the oligarchs to get away with their excesses as well. A system where the courts now must follow the process and which encourages alternative punishments makes a system which is more likely to pursue white collar crimes. A white collar criminal who knows he cannot lose his rights, cannot be put into a prison system so rife with corruption that we now are facing riots, is more likely to agree to an alternate punishment.

Even the most depraved criminal is better than how we treat them. We eliminated Slavery, the consideration of a person as property, over 150 years ago. But we still have this vestige, where we can strip rights from people over petty offenses.

Through making this aspect limited to those who go through a very elaborate process, we limit the abuse of this system and the creation of a new servitude class. And that brings us the nation we all hope to wake up in every morning.

AMENDMENT XIV

Passed by Congress June 13, 1866. Ratified July 9, 1868.

Note: *Article I, section 2, of the Constitution was modified by section 2 of the 14th amendment.*

Section 1.

All persons born or naturalized in the United States, and subject to the jurisdiction thereof, are citizens of the United States and of the State wherein they reside. No State shall make or enforce any law which shall abridge the privileges or immunities of citizens of the United States; nor shall any State deprive any person of life, liberty, or property, without due process of law; nor deny to any person within its jurisdiction the equal protection of the laws.

Section 2.

Representatives shall be apportioned among the several States according to their respective numbers, counting the whole number of persons in each State, excluding Indians not taxed. But when the right to vote at any election for the choice of electors for President and Vice-President of the United States, Representatives in Congress, the Executive and Judicial officers of a State, or the members of the Legislature thereof, is denied to any of the male inhabitants of such State, being twenty-one years of age, and citizens of the United States, or in any way abridged, except for participation in rebellion, or other crime, the basis of representation therein shall be reduced in the proportion which the number of such male citizens shall bear to the whole number of male citizens twenty-one years of age in such State.

Section 3.

No person shall be a Senator or Representative in Congress, or elector of President and Vice-President, or hold any office, civil or military, under the United States, or under any State, who, having previously taken an oath, as a member of Congress, or as an officer of the United States, or as a member of any State legislature, or as an executive or judicial officer of any State, to support the Constitution of the United States, shall have engaged in insurrection or rebellion against the same, or given aid or comfort to the enemies thereof. But Congress may by a vote of two-thirds of each House, remove such disability.

Section 4.

The validity of the public debt of the United States, authorized by law, including debts incurred for payment of pensions and bounties for services in suppressing insurrection or rebellion, shall not be questioned. But neither the United States nor any State shall assume or pay any debt or obligation incurred in aid of insurrection or rebellion against the United States, or any claim for the loss or emancipation of any slave; but all such debts, obligations and claims shall be held illegal and void.

Section 5.

The Congress shall have the power to enforce, by appropriate legislation, the provisions of this article.

Now we have the declaration that all rights are immutable without a legal process, no matter who the person is. This builds upon the 13th Amendment, which overturned indentured servitude laws nationwide. It also means that all laws must be applied equally, which is an area of concern for us today.

Simply put, our laws are not equal by any means. We find racial abuse, discrimination based on prior offenses, and laws designed to benefit the few rather than the many. If a law cannot be used by the majority, then it violates the 14th Amendment on its face, for what else can you call it but deprivation?

And if you note, as mentioned above, Prisoners are not to be counted among a states population for the proportioning of congressional districts. This provision has all but been ignored for over a century, with many states sporting sizable prison populations, yet we do not find the corresponding reduction of the population for congressional redistricting.

Once again, we find a provision which has not had the enforcement upheld. Many states have a current practice of using prisons as population sinks for safe districts. When redistricting, they will seek out prisons for inclusion in legislative districts, aiming to reduce the number of people who can vote for a candidate. This is against the principles of our nation, and must come to an end.

What must happen is that when more people are arrested in each state, the more that state would lose in population for the allocation of representation. And this is clearly marked as an instant system, not one for every 10 years of review.

The problem is that this would make districts as we understand them obsolete, for it would be impractical to redistrict on an annual basis. We must move past the classic district approach to a more pragmatic solution, one based not on a population divided, but on a minimum voting population requirement.

To prevent those who had engineered the Civil War from profiting from the war of the states, or re-entering civil government, this amendment included a provision clearly targeting former officers and elected officials of the Confederacy – prohibiting them from holding elected office in the future. While the Civil War is well over a century and a half in the past, this particular provision does require enforcement even today.

We have succession movements across this country. From Free Vermont to the Republic of Texas, we can witness the detrimental effects of these groups who believe in a fantasy of independent states.

Under this Amendment, so interpreted, candidates such as Sarah Palin or Rick Perry would be banned from holding public office. While their transgressions are little more than rhetoric, the danger lies in letting the topic fester over the long term. But there is no mechanism in place for enforcement at this time, an issue which continues to plague our election systems.

Following the Civil War, there was a serious concern that the United States would default on its debt. This provision set forth that no, the United States could not, under any circumstance, fail to pay its debt.

With the fights over the debt limit, and the government shutdowns, this section has never truly been tested. To be frank, testing it would render even the most hardened lawyer to tears. It is a terrifying thought to put this to the test, for the consequences are that dire.

AMENDMENT XV

Passed by Congress February 26, 1869. Ratified February 3, 1870.

Section 1.
The right of citizens of the United States to vote shall not be denied or abridged by the United States or by any State on account of race, color, or previous condition of servitude--

Section 2.
The Congress shall have the power to enforce this article by appropriate legislation.

The last of the post-Civil War amendments, this one overturned the racially based rights systems which had plagued the United States since it was founded. Sadly, this amendment was all but ignored for over a century, and truly is still ignored.

The rights… shall not be denied or abridged. Very straightforward and simple, yes. This goes on then to specify that they cover this on race, color or previous condition of servitude. Recall the 13th Amendment, that imprisonment is considered a form of servitude, and we can now witness where the issue today begins.

It is now common that ex-convicts find themselves stripped of rights. Many states prohibit those who have served their time from voting. This clearly is not what our Constitution stands for.

Punishment for crimes has already been established to be equal, fair, not cruel, and here it also is set to be term limited. We must accept as a People that once the sentence is over, that is it.

For this to work, we then need to consider the punishment of criminals a moment. Already, we are prohibited from Cruel and Unusual punishment. Now we are tasked to establish that the punishment be brief and absolute. Once the serving out of punishment is completed, it must be considered over with and done.

More than mere interpretation of law, this would mean a complete reassessment of our criminal justice system.

AMENDMENT XVI

Note: Article I, section 9, of the Constitution was modified by amendment 16.

The Congress shall have power to lay and collect taxes on incomes, from whatever source derived, without apportionment among the several States, and without regard to any census or enumeration.

The 16th Amendment, a popular one for the would-be Oligarchs to attack. They attack it because they had succeeded in convincing the courts to interpret taxation their own way, which would have enabled businesses to rob their customers and employees freely and without regard.

You see, they had convinced the court that any and all federal collection had to be through a fixed number, with no ability to adjust based on income. While we popularly consider this for the personal Income Tax, properly its main target were corporate penalties.

Without being able to take into consideration the income of a business, penalizing that business for engaging in illegal activity could only be done either through civil action, or a flat fine. Flat fines of course can either be so high as to instantly destroy any smaller business which is hit, or so low as to be laughable for a major corporate venture.

To address this, the Federal Government implemented fees based on income. It is of note that there was no concern raised over income taxes until the anti-trust actions taken by President Theodore Roosevelt. Suddenly, a huge backlash against income generated taxes and fees appeared as if out of nowhere.

But today, we do not find as much use of the income-based penalties as we once did. Instead we find negotiated settlements, rather than penalties, with corporations able to play their "get out of jail free" cards with impunity. They have no incentive to behave, for there is no true penalty if they fail to follow the rules.

Consider the mountains of coal ash, more radioactive than nuclear waste, which companies just leave in piles. These piles cause people to die every year, thousands of them. Yet, the companies nor those who own and operate them are rarely held liable.

A truly fair system would charge companies as we would a person. If they want corporate personhood, make the corporation stand trial for murder if its products or waste kill someone.

But, as we do not want personhood, the income-derived penalty is the best option. Per death, charge them some fixed percentage, say 10% of their revenue. Not income, revenue. If a dollar comes in, a dime goes out in penalties. In short order, entire industries would go out of business, replaced by those who respect the environment, and safeguard the people of this nation.

Any business which must rely upon not paying the cost of going business must itself go out of business whatever the strategic or economic impact. The damage caused cascades, until it can no longer be validated. But by then, the body count is so massive, admitting the damage becomes impossible.

"Why was nothing done" will be the cry.

"Because we made money at it" is a poor answer.

AMENDMENT XVII

Passed by Congress May 13, 1912. Ratified April 8, 1913.

Note: *Article I, section 3, of the Constitution was modified by the 17th amendment.*

The Senate of the United States shall be composed of two Senators from each State, elected by the people thereof, for six years; and each Senator shall have one vote. The electors in each State shall have the qualifications requisite for electors of the most numerous branch of the State legislatures.

With this passage, Senators became elected, rather than mere appointments by the state legislatures. This move helped transition the Senate from an undemocratic body to one better fitting our Republic. How the Senators are elected is specified as being through the same method used for the state legislatures. This does not mean that it is guaranteed a democracy, but it does mean that the system which had been in place, which was rife with abuse and corruption, was replaced. States could pick their Senators only through whatever process is used for their own legislature, so anything done to change their Senator election process would then be applied on themselves. Even with this change, the method used in all states at this time still has one critical flaw.

The Senate seats are elected independent of one another, directly.

As discussed earlier, these kinds of elections leads to unrepresentative results, and party politic dominance. Again, not what our founders intended, and clearly not what we need today. Thankfully the solution is far simpler than for the House of Representatives.

Elect both seats in a single election, using proportional voting, such as Single Transferable Voting (described later).

Unlike the house, which is redistricted regularly, the US Senate is based on whole states as a single body. There is, based on prior restriction put in to our Constitution, little risk of us seeing North and South Dakota merging, or of California splitting into numerous other states. A state's border and territory are effectively frozen in place.

This makes such a proportional system ideal for use, while also eliminating much of the party control over the process. Even if there are only two seats, the lack of regular, or any, redistricting, eliminates the main concern over proportional systems which only have such few seats elected.

And, the beauty is, the US Constitution already provided this for us in its language. It states that the Senators will be elected by the people, but groups the two together. Two seats unified implies one election.

By doing so, we have rendered the Senate a more representative body for the states from which our Senators are to serve. And representation is precisely what it is the Senators need to do.

When vacancies happen in the representation of any State in the Senate, the executive authority of such State shall issue writs of election to fill such vacancies: Provided, That the legislature of any State may empower the executive thereof to make temporary appointments until the people fill the vacancies by election as the legislature may direct.

If a Senator must vacate their position, be it for any reason, the state's governor is to call for an election to replace them. In the meantime, the legislature may grant permission to the governor to appoint someone to fill in until that special election is held. A simple and practical solution rooted in the previous methodology of appointing Senators.

Elections take time to organize, time to execute. During this time, a state could be left without suitable representation. That would never do, so the most direct method available is the one chosen — to enable the previous Senator appointment system to continue *in this one scenario.*

By doing so, the state would maintain its voice, and the government could continue to operate.

This amendment shall not be so construed as to affect the election or term of any Senator chosen before it becomes valid as part of the Constitution.

This is only historical now. It was included so as to tell the current Senators that they would continue to fill out their time in the Senate until the next elections arrived. It meant a continuing of station, and ensured stability during this transition.

Today, this provision is meaningless. Even the newest Senator upon the day it passed would have been up for election in 1920. By now, this time period is almost a century behind us, so is now a historical leftover, like the appendix.

That said, it serves to remind us of how our Constitution forbade retroactive applications of law. Just as we cannot retroactively make something a crime, nor can we retroactively change how elections are handled. As such, any adjustments to Senate or Representatives must be handled in the next elections, and do not apply to any prior.

AMENDMENT XVIII

Passed by Congress December 18, 1917. Ratified January 16, 1919. Repealed by amendment 21.

Section 1.
After one year from the ratification of this article the manufacture, sale, or transportation of intoxicating liquors within, the importation thereof into, or the exportation thereof from the United States and all territory subject to the jurisdiction thereof for beverage purposes is hereby prohibited.

Section 2.
The Congress and the several States shall have concurrent power to enforce this article by appropriate legislation.

The grand idea, Prohibition.

A grand failure. This is a warning for all, that the use of the Constitution for legislation is itself a mistake. The Constitution is designed as a framework, not a law. By the use of the Constitution to force legislation, and behavior upon society, the result was a complete and utter failure.

Rather than liquor vanishing, it became a status symbol, and the root of criminal activity. The backfiring of this Amendment, swept in by a vocal minority and misguided use of public opinion, should serve as a lesson not just as to how the Amendment process can be abused, but precisely why the process is as complicated as it is.

Section 3.
This article shall be inoperative unless it shall have been ratified as an amendment to the Constitution by the legislatures of the several States, as provided in the Constitution, within seven years from the date of the submission hereof to the States by the Congress.

Here is where the amendment is more interesting. For this amendment, they included a section on ratification. But, if the amendment was not passed, this section would not take effect. A Catch 22 situation.

The idea here of course is to have a term limit for the implementation of Amendments. The problem is, the provision does not apply without ratification in the first place.

So not only did the 18th Amendment introduce a bad policy, but it added a bad precedent. By us acting as if these expiration dates had any weight, we gave them weight. We need to stop including them, and even review those Amendments which failed to gain full passage before their time expired. Since their expiry is itself not yet ratified, they can still be passed today.

No, if we want a "due by" for Amendments, it would require a special amendment in and of itself. Since no such amendment has been passed, we must disregard these..

AMENDMENT XIX

Passed by Congress June 4, 1919. Ratified August 18, 1920.

The right of citizens of the United States to vote shall not be denied or abridged by the United States or by any State on account of sex.

Congress shall have power to enforce this article by appropriate legislation.

What we have here is a promise of equality in the ballot box regardless of gender. This becomes very important with the current issues surrounding LGBT equality. Universal suffrage was a challenge which still has not been fully resolved.

Before the 19th Amendment, women were second class citizens at best, property at worst. Homosexuals, transgendered, etc were even worse. While until 1860, we can find plenty of examples of LGBT equality, by 1880 it was almost universally banned across the United States.

With the 19th Amendment, here we do not see a statement on women directly, but instead the lifting of right restrictions. Already, the 15th Amendment had removed racially based restrictions. With the 19th Amendment, everyone, be it women, transgendered, homosexual, what have you, now had full rights.

Ultimately, the power of the ballot box is the supreme power of the land, and therefore the most important right there is. As with the 15th Amendment eliminating the barriers, in theory, for people based on race, the 19th Amendment broke the glass ceiling for those who were not straight, male, eliminating second class status.

Once the right to vote is there, all other rights and privileges of citizenship are implied, for otherwise that right to vote is meaningless.

AMENDMENT XX

Passed by Congress March 2, 1932. Ratified January 23, 1933.

Note: *Article I, section 4, of the Constitution was modified by section 2 of this amendment. In addition, a portion of the 12th amendment was superseded by section 3.*

Section 1.
The terms of the President and the Vice President shall end at noon on the 20th day of January, and the terms of Senators and Representatives at noon on the 3d day of January, of the years in which such terms would have ended if this article had not been ratified; and the terms of their successors shall then begin.

Section 2.
The Congress shall assemble at least once in every year, and such meeting shall begin at noon on the 3d day of January, unless they shall by law appoint a different day.

Section 3.
If, at the time fixed for the beginning of the term of the President, the President elect shall have died, the Vice President elect shall become President. If a President shall not have been chosen before the time fixed for the beginning of his term, or if the President elect shall have failed to qualify, then the Vice President elect shall act as President until a President shall have qualified; and the Congress may by law provide for the case wherein neither a President elect nor a Vice President elect shall have qualified, declaring who shall then act as President, or the manner in which one who is to act shall be selected, and such person shall act accordingly until a President or Vice President shall have qualified.

Section 4.
The Congress may by law provide for the case of the death of any of the persons from whom the House of Representatives may choose a President whenever the right of choice shall have devolved upon them, and for the case of the death of any of the persons from whom the Senate may choose a Vice President whenever the right of choice shall have devolved upon them.

Section 5.
Sections 1 and 2 shall take effect on the 15th day of October following the ratification of this article.

Section 6.
This article shall be inoperative unless it shall have been ratified as an amendment to the Constitution by the legislatures of three-fourths of the several States within seven years from the date of its submission.

With modern technology making the long process of certifying elections now obsolete, Congress moved to reduce the time between the election of officers, and the taking of office, to half what it was, sufficient to handle the handing over of power.

It also put into place a provision to address the issue of a president-elect who passes before they take office. There had been several close calls, after all. It also reset the day in which Congress would begin its session.

But more importantly, it affirmed the role in which Congress has in the selection of the President – that it is Congress, not the People, who have to pick the President should the unforeseen occur.

This almost was tested in 1933, when a cabal of America's richest men began the preparation for a putsch against President Roosevelt. It was only for their attempt to recruit General Smedley Butler which foiled their plans.

The plan would have relied upon the lack of provisions found within this amendment, to have inserted a military figurehead, either Butler or the next choice of General Douglass MacArthur, with the legislature having no alternative but to affirm the chosen leader. Nearly overnight, a democracy would have been replaced with a fascist totalitarian regime.

This Amendment neutered such an effort by putting a more concrete inheritance, so should the unimaginable happen, there would have been a clear chain of inheritance of presidential election.

The "Wall Street Putsch" shocked a core segment of our politicians into action. While all but forgotten today, it remains a black mark on our democracy, reminding us all that democracy is under threat by moneyed interests, who would put capitalism itself before the voice of the People.

AMENDMENT XXI

Passed by Congress February 20, 1933. Ratified December 5, 1933.

Section 1.
The eighteenth article of amendment to the Constitution of the United States is hereby repealed.

Section 2.
The transportation or importation into any State, Territory, or possession of the United States for delivery or use therein of intoxicating liquors, in violation of the laws thereof, is hereby prohibited.

Section 3.
This article shall be inoperative unless it shall have been ratified as an amendment to the Constitution by conventions in the several States, as provided in the Constitution, within seven years from the date of the submission hereof to the States by the Congress.

And so ended Prohibition. By legislating through the Amendment process, our nation made a judgmental error of severe proportions. Prohibition saw the rise of organized crime, and a police state which has only grown since.

AMENDMENT XXII

Section 1.

No person shall be elected to the office of the President more than twice, and no person who has held the office of President, or acted as President, for more than two years of a term to which some other person was elected President shall be elected to the office of the President more than once. But this Article shall not apply to any person holding the office of President when this Article was proposed by the Congress, and shall not prevent any person who may be holding the office of President, or acting as President, during the term within which this Article becomes operative from holding the office of President or acting as President during the remainder of such term.

Section 2.

This article shall be inoperative unless it shall have been ratified as an amendment to the Constitution by the legislatures of three-fourths of the several States within seven years from the date of its submission to the States by the Congress.

After Present Franklin Roosevelt's historical 4 terms in office, there was a solid concern over an "Imperial Presidency" forming. Being in office for so long would mean one person would have an undue influence over the nation. In answer to this, the decision was made to formalize the tradition set forth by President George Washington, to limit the president to no more than two terms of office.

That they felt the need to enact such an amendment speaks volumes of the fear held by some politicians in this nation. They feared unchecked power, but also of political party domination. Roosevelt had in effect made his Democratic party the sole party of power within the United States. The Republican party was gutted by the changes he pushed through.

With his death in 1945, and President Truman's failure with domestic policies, the Republicans used the opportunity to gain a majority in congress, and used that unpopularity to pass this amendment.

The result has been, in all honesty, nothing special. While there had been talk of revoking it for popular presidents such as Reagan and Clinton, neither men felt up to another four years in the White House. Indeed, the amendment may have done more to prolong their lives than anything else.

But do term limits achieve the desired result? The idea was to prevent a single person from dominating politics. But in so doing, we have diminished the impact from the Presidency.

Now any President can misbehave during his second term, for there is no penalty in so doing. Declare that a measure of Congress gives the ability to invade a random country, no problem. Revoke regulations which protect our economy from collapse, piece of cake. We have turned the Presidents second term into the opportunity to form a true Imperial Presidency.

One interesting piece of exclusion is the office of the Vice President. Having divorced it from the Executive branch, and turned into a Prime Minister style position, the Vice

President can be a continual, stable force in government. So long as the powers as the Head of State and Head of Government remain solidly behind the President however, the fear of the Imperial Presidency remain. This divorce of authority will address the creeping authority, and help see the United States continue for centuries into the culture.

Yet, despite the obvious avenue for corruption which term limits bring, we have those who would seek to expand term limits to congress as well. This would turn our legislature into an audition for the Oligarchs to select their preferred pets. Rather than giving us the best government in the world, the use of term limits would instead guarantee us the worst of the worst – those who would have nothing to gain for doing their jobs, and everything to gain for not.

Instead, we need to look at our legislators as those we want to reward. In the past, we promised fat pensions and post-retirement bonuses. It is time we built upon those, but with strings attached. For those who served our government who then work for agencies that then rely upon the government, lobbyists in other words, they would find those benefits cut off. That is the most assured way for which we are to only select the best and brightest as our politicians.

Someone serves in Congress for one term, they gain a small pension. As they serve more time, perhaps in the House, then the Senate, before eventually rising to a Cabinet position, these pension benefits gather. This then means once they do leave office, perhaps after 30 years of public service, there is now a serious incentive to not become a lobbyist, or to use their connections for personal gain.

It may seem contradictory, but it does add up once you begin to consider the implications. Those with a single 2-year term would have far fewer connections than those with dozens of years within the beltway. Therefore, their ability to serve as a lobbying agent is reduced as well.

Seniority brings with it connections, and it is those connections we need to prevent from falling into the evil hands of the Oligarchs.

AMENDMENT XXIII

Passed by Congress June 16, 1960. Ratified March 29, 1961.

Section 1.
The District constituting the seat of Government of the United States shall appoint in such manner as the Congress may direct:

A number of electors of President and Vice President equal to the whole number of Senators and Representatives in Congress to which the District would be entitled if it were a State, but in no event more than the least populous State; they shall be in addition to those appointed by the States, but they shall be considered, for the purposes of the election of President and Vice President, to be electors appointed by a State; and they shall meet in the District and perform such duties as provided by the twelfth article of amendment.

Section 2.
The Congress shall have power to enforce this article by appropriate legislation.

The 23rd amendment gave the nation's capital a voice in electing the president. But, it gives something more. Since the provision enabling the United States is intertwined with the establishment of the seat of government, this Amendment can be considered to be applicable to the various territories.

But further, as it specifies that these electors would be in addition to those appointed by the states, and that the 12th amendment would integrate them in the same manner as those electors, this would in turn grant representation in the lower house, where these electors meet, to these territories.

These territories, if you'd recall, included everything from the District of Columbia to the Native reservations. It specifies here that these agencies may have no more seats than electors to the least populous state, so no more than 3. As this would only define them as having membership in the lower house, the House of Representatives, but not to the Senate, this would give a voice, even if an imperfect one, to populations currently disenfranchised by our system of government.

By granting territories electors for President, and by having these electors already established as tied to representation, there is no Constitutional manner by which these districts or territories can be denied representation within the House of Representatives. It will be limited compared to a full state, being only of the lower house and with a maximum representative count of 3, but it would meet the obligations as set forth within our Constitution.

A further amendment, granting these non-states a single Senator, would help even more. But that is beyond the scope of what this amendment could provide, no matter how far we extrapolate it.

AMENDMENT XXIV

Passed by Congress August 27, 1962. Ratified January 23, 1964.

Section 1.
The right of citizens of the United States to vote in any primary or other election for President or Vice President, for electors for President or Vice President, or for Senator or Representative in Congress, shall not be denied or abridged by the United States or any State by reason of failure to pay any poll tax or other tax.

Section 2.
The Congress shall have power to enforce this article by appropriate legislation.

A tactic by which the People are disenfranchised is by applying tests, be it of wealth or literacy or any other fanciful tests the Oligarchs could imagine. It is not in their best interest to have the rabble believing they had any say in their governance, after all.

The 24th Amendment eliminated the ability to deny or abridge the right to vote based on these common tactics. But it did something else as well, far more subtle.

By declaring the right to vote independent of any tax, poll or otherwise, it eliminated the effort by some to limit voting to wealthy landowners. Now even the poorest person within the United States would have a say in their representation. This has not sat well with the would be Oligarchs, who would prefer that only those who they deem worthy, namely the wealthy and powerful, would carry any voice in government.

AMENDMENT XXV

Passed by Congress July 6, 1965. Ratified February 10, 1967.

Note: *Article II, section 1, of the Constitution was affected by the 25th amendment.*

Section 1.
In case of the removal of the President from office or of his death or resignation, the Vice President shall become President.

Section 2.
Whenever there is a vacancy in the office of the Vice President, the President shall nominate a Vice President who shall take office upon confirmation by a majority vote of both Houses of Congress.

Section 3.
Whenever the President transmits to the President pro tempore of the Senate and the Speaker of the House of Representatives his written declaration that he is unable to discharge the powers and duties of his office, and until he transmits to them a written declaration to the contrary, such powers and duties shall be discharged by the Vice President as Acting President.

Section 4.
Whenever the Vice President and a majority of either the principal officers of the executive departments or of such other body as Congress may by law provide, transmit to the President pro tempore of the Senate and the Speaker of the House of Representatives their written declaration that the President is unable to discharge the powers and duties of his office, the Vice President shall immediately assume the powers and duties of the office as Acting President.

Thereafter, when the President transmits to the President pro tempore of the Senate and the Speaker of the House of Representatives his written declaration that no inability exists, he shall resume the powers and duties of his office unless the Vice President and a majority of either the principal officers of the executive department or of such other body as Congress may by law provide, transmit within four days to the President pro tempore of the Senate and the Speaker of the House of Representatives their written declaration that the President is unable to discharge the powers and duties of his office. Thereupon Congress shall decide the issue, assembling within forty-eight hours for that purpose if not in session. If the Congress, within twenty-one days after receipt of the latter written declaration, or, if Congress is not in session, within twenty-one days after Congress is required to assemble, determines by two-thirds vote of both Houses that the President is unable to discharge the powers and duties of his office, the Vice President shall continue to discharge the same as Acting President; otherwise, the President shall resume the powers and duties of his office.

We take it for granted that should a Vice President take over for the President that he would become President, but it was never spelled out in the Constitution. Starting with President Tyler, when the Vice President took over the duties of the President, he also gained the title of President. There was a considerable amount of debate on this topic, until finally with the death of President Kennedy putting Lyndon Johnson in to the White House the nation decided on formalizing what had been a de facto standard.

When the Vice President was forced to assume the office of President, it left a gap in the chain of command. Who took over as Vice President. At varying points, the US Senate elected them, and at other points they had no Vice President at all.

By enabling the incoming President to select his replacement as Vice President, this set down a firm directive for who would fill this role once and for all. But this was not an arbitrary decision. Both houses of Congress have to approve of the decision. This confirms the checks and balances system which has been inherent in the Constitution from the beginning.

In case the President becomes temporarily incapacitated, we now have a new option put forth here, that of an Acting President. The first avenue by which this action can be taken would be for the President himself to formally petition the Senate. A President needing to go for surgery, one in grief, or even one who just needs a vacation from the pressures of the job, has the option to file with Congress that the Vice President shall act in their stead until he decides otherwise.

The next avenue by which a President can be temporarily replaced, with the Vice President stepping in as Acting President is if the Vice President and a majority of the cabinet file with Congress that the President is unable to discharge the powers and duties of the office. As before, the petition must be filed with Congress. However here there is an interesting note in that Congress is enabled to create laws detailing out a variety of avenues by which the President would be considered unable to perform in office.

Now, should the President be ruled incapacitated in this manner, he can fight it. However the process by which he can regain office is not straightforward. For one, Congress does not have to vote on restoring the President for three weeks. To continue keeping the President out of his office requires a super-majority vote, but a clever Parliamentarian could easily arrange delay after delay, and abuse the process in order to keep a President from office.

This is an avenue by which a President who has not committed a crime, but is compromised from performing their duty effectively can be addressed. It becomes an emergency system, enabling the country to continue operation no matter what. It also adds an intermediate step between full duty and impeachment.

Congress however has never properly explored their duties under this amendment however. To date, it has only been used for a handful of emergencies, such as when President Reagan was shot. The most extreme emergency has not yet happened, but it is possible that some day in the future Congress may see a need to use these powers.

Consider the application of this power as the counterpoint to the President's power to dismiss Congress. This makes both able to effectively disable the other, but in so doing also undercut their own ability to function. Congress can put the Vice President into power as well as remove the President entirely, while the President can only suspend. A firm reminder as to whom is in the drivers seat of our nation – Congress and noone else.

AMENDMENT XXVI

Passed by Congress March 23, 1971. Ratified July 1, 1971.

Note: *Amendment 14, section 2, of the Constitution was modified by section 1 of the 26th amendment.*

Section 1.
The right of citizens of the United States, who are eighteen years of age or older, to vote shall not be denied or abridged by the United States or by any State on account of age.

An inconsistent age at which we considered adulthood resulted in what was widely viewed as an injustice. We were sending young men to fight, and die, in the forests of Vietnam to prop up the puppet state of South Vietnam, while denying them the right to a say in their governance at home.

To resolve this, the 26th Amendment made the voting age uniform nationwide, at 18. By doing so, we codified something which was understood for centuries before, that the People were to have the final say. "No Taxation Without Representation" takes on new meaning when one considers the sacrifices our military men and women a form of taxation.

Section 2.
The Congress shall have power to enforce this article by appropriate legislation.

As before, Congress is charged to pass laws to reflect this Amendment.

AMENDMENT XXVII

Originally proposed Sept. 25, 1789. Ratified May 7, 1992.

No law, varying the compensation for the services of the Senators and Representatives, shall take effect, until an election of Representatives shall have intervened.

Originally drafted as part of the Bill of Rights, the 27th Amendment sat in limbo for most of our nations history. It codified something important, that legislation involving a member of congress' salary could not take effect until the following Congress. Or rather, that is how it is interpreted.

But, there's a comma, right after "No Law" which makes me pause for a moment. If this were passed in the 18th century, the case could be made that it was an eccentricity of language. But it was passed in the 20th, written as is, which tells us that the actual root sentence is "No Law shall take effect, until an election of Representatives shall have intervened." The second part then, "varying the compensation for the services of the Senators and Representatives" is being handled independently of other bills. And indeed, earlier in the Constitution we find that indeed there is a provision detailing out their compensation, with one section, for the president, to be done only at the end of his elected period.

So how do we use this section? If Congress were to have a Presidential adjustment of salary, to run for each elected term, Senators would only have a pay raise every 6 years. This would not do. Instead, our tradition has the president and congress having compensation tied to each other. However even then, the concern with pay adjustment was a large one, and now congress has its salary adjusted every year using a cost of living adjustment automatically generated. This was set by the Ethics Reform Act of 1989, and now found in Pub.L. 101-194 . Which mean either the Ethics Reform Act is unconstitutional, if the 27th Amendment is to be taken as only applying to compensation, or it is fully constitutional if it does not.

In truth, the interpretation that the 27th amendment only applies to the passage of laws save those dealing with congressional compensation is the most rational. It prevents the kind of hostage taking and shutdowns we have witnessed these past several decades. As any such measure, including monetary expenditures, would not take effect until the following congressional session, it would be a significantly more elaborate, and self-destructive tactic to try. Now, going in to elections, rather than hiding issues by spending short term spending bills, the people would know that the existing congress people were playing politics with shutdown. Combine with a more representative STV voting method, this would be political suicide for anyone attempting to shut down the country.

As this amendment was written by our founders, even if not implemented until modern times, the interpretation of it is up to us, lacking any real history to build upon. And as such, we must ensure that Congress follows what is laid out, in simple black and white.

UNRATIFIED AMENDMENTS

There have been several proposed amendments to the Constitution which have, for one reason or another, not been ratified. To date, there have been 6 amendments which have been passed by Congress, but have not as of yet been ratified by the states.

Some of these amendments date back to the very founding of our nation. Some cover topics no longer considered a concern. Other ones have been addressed through legislative means. One was addressed with a civil war.

Now we shall review these could-be amendments, and discuss how they can be adapted to suit our needs if ever passed. Some, admittedly, are so tied to the era they were written, that they simply no longer make any sense to ratify at all.

CONGRESSIONAL APPORTIONMENT AMENDMENT

After the first enumeration required by the first article of the Constitution, there shall be one Representative for every thirty thousand, until the number shall amount to one hundred, after which the proportion shall be so regulated by Congress, that there shall be not less than one hundred Representatives, nor less than one Representative for every forty thousand persons, until the number of Representatives shall amount to two hundred; after which the proportion shall be so regulated by Congress, that there shall not be less than two hundred Representatives, nor more than one Representative for every fifty thousand persons.

Now, this amendment changes how congress is allocated. How we allocate congressional seats today is that Congress sets how many members of Congress there are, and then divide that among the states based on population. This results in situations where Wyoming, with 563,626 people according to the 2010 census, having the same number of representatives as Montana, despite the latter state having nearly double the population. So instead, this amendment put a minimum number for both seats in Congress, and changed the allocation not by setting the number of congressional seats and then dividing up based on that, but instead based congressional apportion on maximum district population and minimum number of seats.

However, the included math from the amendment is dated. If we used the metrics put down here, our House of Representatives would sit at 6,174 members. This is completely unworkable, clearly.

Another way to interpret this amendment is that it sets up a model for growth. The number of representatives is set not from the top down, by Congress, but from the bottom-up, by population. So let us continue this trend. At its peak, it has 200 representatives at 50,000 people each, or 10 million people. The United States hit this population point in 1820. Once we hit 300 representatives, it would go to 60,000 people. That grows to a population of 18 million, which the US passed in the census of 1850.

Continuing the trend, 400 representatives at 70,000 people, 28 million people passed in 1860. 500 representatives at 80,000 people, 40 million people, passed in 1880. 600 representatives at 90,000 people, 54 million people, passed in 1890. And so forth.

If this system continued, we would have today 1,817 members of the House of Representatives, each one representing no more than 170,000 people. As well, the house would have to have a minimum of 1800 legislators. This, clearly, is not viable for good governance.

However, the important part is not the numbers directly, but in how the house is proportioned. Rather than setting a number of representatives, then calculating out the number to divide the population, you apportion based on a basic, minimum number of people. Then you have a minimum number of representatives in the house, to prevent under-representation.

When this Amendment was first proposed, the smallest territory by population was Tennessee, at 35,691. Hence, the basic unit was 30,000. So, let us use this same approach. This would mean only one state, the smallest, would have only 1 representative. Take the population of the smallest state, round down to the nearest 10,000 in population, and use that as the basic unit of a district, and for allocation. Then, we take this basic unit size, divide the overall population of the United States by it, round down to the nearest 100's, and we will then have the minimum number of representatives.

Returning to our lest populous state of Wyoming, our unit size using this model would come to 560,000. Every representative seat would then need to be apportioned according to the population with no districts above 560,000 rounded down, and with no fewer than 500 representatives. Going down the list of states, this is the number of seats each would be apportioned:

STATE	Cur. No. Rep	New Number
Alabama	7	9
Alaska	1	2
Arizona	9	12
Arkansas	4	6
California	53	67
Colorado	7	9
Connecticut	5	7
Delaware	1	2
Florida	27	34
Georgia	14	18
Hawaii	2	3
Idaho	2	3
Illinois	18	23
Indiana	9	12
Iowa	4	6
Kansas	4	6
Kentucky	6	8
Louisiana	6	9
Maine	2	3
Maryland	8	11
Massachusetts	9	12
Michigan	14	18
Minnesota	8	10
Mississippi	4	6
Missouri	8	11
Montana	1	2
Nebraska	3	4
Nevada	4	5
New Hampshire	2	3
New Jersey	12	16
New Mexico	3	4
New York	27	35
North Carolina	13	18
North Dakota	1	2
Ohio	16	21
Oklahoma	5	7
Oregon	5	7
Pennsylvania	18	23
Rhode Island	2	2
South Carolina	7	9
South Dakota	1	2
Tennessee	9	12
Texas	36	45
Utah	4	5
Vermont	1	2
Virginia	11	15
Washington	10	12
West Virginia	3	4
Wisconsin	8	11
Wyoming	1	1
TOTAL	435	574

As you can see, this apportioning method, being based on rounding down from the ten-thousand space, results in overall more seats in Congress. Once combined with the multi-seat districts from STV, the proportional approach discussed earlier, this would make both for far simpler districting and for a more representative government.

One of the challenges in modern redistricting is in making sure each district is exactly equal. This approach, with a minimum number of seats, and maximum population, means that districts no longer need to be perfectly the same size. This grants the flexibility for use of existing borders, rather than needing to create often times crazy districts to maintain cohesive populations.

As such, should this Amendment ever pass, it would only enhance the existing system which we have laid out, further strengthening our democracy over the longer term.

TITLES OF NOBILITY AMENDMENT

If any citizen of the United States shall accept, claim, receive or retain, any title of nobility or honour, or shall, without the consent of Congress, accept and retain any present, pension, office or emolument of any kind whatever, from any emperor, king, prince or foreign power, such person shall cease to be a citizen of the United States, and shall be incapable of holding any office of trust or profit under them, or either of them

Building upon Article I, Section 9, this Amendment would strip the citizenship for anyone who was part of a foreign power. This would, if adopted, change the dynamic over relationships with foreign nations, and would block a number of office holders going forward.

There is, interestingly, little wiggle room for interpretation. If someone were to work for a foreign power, they would lose their US citizenship. This leaves a large gray area however, for it specifies 'foreign power' and not 'foreign government' as one would expect.

On the surface, the amendment would prohibit working for a foreign owned company, for example. This would be a major issue for those who work for US affiliates of foreign corporations. An "us vs them" nationalist mentality could abuse such an amendment in an extreme manner, by stripping the rights from any and all who could benefit from foreign goods and services. As written, this amendment would make it nearly impossible for foreign owned companies to to business, or even operate within the United States.

As such, this amendment would be foolish to pass, as it would only bring harm. The isolationism which it is rooted on is so anachronistic today it is almost laughable. However, there remain those who would seek to ratify it, so we must be wary.

CORWIN AMENDMENT

No amendment shall be made to the Constitution which will authorize or give to Congress the power to abolish or interfere, within any State, with the domestic institutions thereof, including that of persons held to labor or service by the laws of said State.

The brainchild of Representative Thomas Corwin of Ohio, this amendment was a last, desperate attempt to stop the looming civil war over slavery. It is likely one of the most illogical amendments ever passed. It was an amendment which forbade amendments that impacted "domestic institutions". If we went by the manner in which it was written, it makes no sense , unless you were let in on the little secret that they meant slavery.

However, modern domestic institutions are very different from those of 1860. No longer do we have slavery to contend with. But states still have institutions, specifically the branches of their government.

By not stating slavery itself, but only inferring it, the Corwin Amendment as/is leaves itself wide open for interpretation. This amendment if passed today would mean effectively whatever it is we wished it to.

A use for it could be to prevent federal shutdown of state governments. While no such federal takeover of state functions has occurred in a long time, the authority to do so remains in place. But this is a major stretch of ability.

In more practical terms, it would severely limit the power of Article V for the states to pass amendments. It could even be argued that it would strip states of the power to form Article V conventions at all, effectively railroading the amending process while also limiting what could be done.

It would be the ultimate form of "States Rights" in print. Any state could claim some role, function or law an "institution" and shut down any federal amendment, law or regulation to limit it – even if it did not exist beforehand.

How it could be applied directly without much stretch would be to empower states to impact each other. One state allowing companies to pollute water which flowed into neighboring states, and nothing could be done about it, for example. Another would be to drop off prisoners in another state, and dump them for someone else to deal with.

The ways in which this could be abused are numerous, and rather terrifying to consider. As a result, any attempt to ratify this amendment would grossly backfire should it be attempted. This is an unratified amendment which needs to be left to the history books. It does no good to us today, and would only serve to undermine the nation itself.

CHILD LABOR AMENDMENT

Section 1. *The Congress shall have power to limit, regulate, and prohibit the labor of persons under eighteen years of age.*

Section 2. *The power of the several States is unimpaired by this article except that the operation of State laws shall be suspended to the extent necessary to give effect to legislation enacted by the Congress.*

The concern over child labor was strong in the late 19th century. Factories employed the underaged in often times dangerous conditions, where familial poverty forced all members into the workforce. There were whole orphanages set up for the exploitation of those under their care. Early attempts to regulate the use of child labor through the tax code, such as the Child Labor Tax Law of 1919 and the Keating-Owen Child Labor Act of 1916, were overturned by the Supreme court due to an unequal application of taxation (CLTL) and the use of the commerce clause to add an undue barrier to interstate commerce (KOCLA). Congress responded by passing this amendment. It would make a uniform standard for child labor across the US, rather than leaving it up to the various states.

However, with the passing of the Fair Labor Standards Act of 1938, the need for this amendment has been eliminated. By passing the FLSA, the court found that Congress had given itself the proper tools for regulating labor had been given while before Congress was engaging in tricks to dance around the lack of such a framework. This enables the restriction of labor for those under the age of majority.

If passed today, this amendment would do little to nothing directly. However, it would be a moral victory for us as a nation, telling the world that no, children are not to be used for personal gain – that their childhood is for learning, growing into adulthood where they can make the choice for their own future.

EQUAL RIGHTS AMENDMENT

Section 1. Equality of rights under the law shall not be denied or abridged by the United States or by any State on account of sex.

Section 2. The Congress shall have the power to enforce, by appropriate legislation, the provisions of this article.

Section 3. This amendment shall take effect two years after the date of ratification.

Sexism and bigotry is still a major issue within the United States. The Equal Rights Amendment was passed in order to help address this issue. But without ratification, this final step for equality of gender is left undone.

The way it is written, this amendment would outlaw anti-abortion laws, restrictions on those who are transgender, even the ban on gay men donating blood. These laws do target based on sex, be it a persons gender, their biology, or their sexual orientation.

As such, this amendment should be ratified by the states.

DISTRICT OF COLUMBIA VOTING RIGHTS AMENDMENT

Section 1. For purposes of representation in the Congress, election of the President and Vice President, and article V of this Constitution, the District constituting the seat of government of the United States shall be treated as though it were a State.

Section 2. The exercise of the rights and powers conferred under this article shall be by the people of the District constituting the seat of government, and as shall be provided by the Congress.

Section 3. The twenty-third article of amendment to the Constitution of the United States is hereby repealed.

Section 4. This article shall be inoperative, unless it shall have been ratified as an amendment to the Constitution by the legislatures of three-fourths of the several States within seven years from the date of its submission.

This amendment would serve to help grant the District of Columbia proper representation within our government. At this time, D.C. effectively lacks representation. This amendment would not, however, make D.C. a state, and would only grant them the equivalent electoral college representation as if they were a state only for purposes of electing the President.

This however only gives this power to D.C. itself, and not any of the other territories still held by the United States. While D.C. is important, it cannot be granted importance over the voices otherwise silenced.

A motion to grant full representation in the house divided up by the territories directly would instead be the right solution. With the population holding representation, they would hold a say that they currently lack. But note, no Senator is being discussed here. The House of Representatives is there to represent the people as a whole is why, while the Senate is based on statehood. This setup would give a voice, for taxation with representation, while holding a carrot out for the territories who decide to pursue statehood.

OPTIONS FOR DEMOCRACY

At this time, the existing manner in which we interpret the Constitutional framework within the United States is classically called a Representative, or Liberal Democracy. There are several forms of this, from Jacksonian Democracy to a Parliamentary Democracy. The underlying concept remains the same, people elect the officials to serve in higher office through some mechanism, and the elected officials then enforce the law while protecting the rights of the people. A very simple concept.

However, other aspects of traditional Liberal Democracies have come with problems. For example, elections are primarily viewed as competitive events, with distinct winners and losers, similar to sporting events. Liberal Democracies all but require the use political parties for elections, resulting in what develops into a "loyal opposition." By itself, these two aspects are not bad, but under the right circumstances, they can develop into a nightmare.

The competitive nature of the democratic process results in Liberal Democracies becoming less capable of serving as an extension of the People. People who witness those they support losing too often begin to disengage. Just look at the fans of sports teams which have not gone to a prestigious event for long periods. The term Fairweather Johnson exists to describe this block of supporters who only appear when a particular team or athlete is doing well.

This fear of loss then creates an incentive to take every advantage possible. Much like an athlete being tempted to take performance enhancing drugs, politicians will be tempted to solicit funds for a war chest to tackle their opposition. And the small pool of funds available would then encourage the most bang for the buck, which in elections is the negative campaign. Funds however often come with strings. And so the would be Oligarchy gains their foothold into the system. Instead of focusing on yourself, you focus on flaws, real or imagined, of your opponent, in order to dishearten their supporters. And when you win, you have both managed to dissuade voter participation, and now owe your success to those who do not necessarily have the People's best interests in mind.

Clearly, this is not sustainable. And with voter turnout continuing to fall, eventually it will not be.

One commonly cited option to address the issues within our government is to take an approach used in other nations which use a parliament, that of proportional representation. We can adapt the principles of a parliament to fit the framework included within the Constitution. But this only would introduce the problems of a Parliament, without properly addressing the more overriding issue at hand.

Instead, let us break down the core elements of our nation's political framework, and see what we have to build on.

First, let us take a look back at Article I, and the concept of Electors. The founders never called them voters, after all, but instead used a category for them alone. As such, the definition of an Elector can and would change over time. And they left that definition not up to the federal government, but to the states. As such, the standards for one state may not match that of another.

By enabling this, our founders expected for the states to experiment with democracy, to create new systems and refine old ones. As solutions worked, they would be more broadly adapted. When they did not, they would be abandoned.

Somewhere along the lines, we forgot this simple fact, that while the federal government is in charge, it is built using discrete elements, not a monolithic structure. Our differences are what make our nation stronger.

There are of course civic protections in place however. A state cannot, for example, limit voting to just men, or of members from a particular ethnic group, due to various Amendments to the Constitution. But it can decide on how the votes are counted or allotted, so long as every vote is given equal standing.

The issues we need to address are numerous. We need to address the issue of gerrymandering. We need to address the issue of party dominance over the electoral system. We need to address the issue of money dominance in our political process. We need to address the issue of our elected officials not reflecting the people which they are there to serve. We need to address the issue of voter apathy. And we need to address the issue of elected officials being able to do the jobs for which they were appointed by the voters.

And, if we dive down, all of these elements are not by design, but are an accident based on the voting method we adopted early on, First Past the Post, or FPTP.

Under an FPTP system, the winner is whomever received the most votes, even if that person did not win a majority of support. This results in a situation where the more candidates are running for any particular office will result in a smaller number of votes are needed to win. In a three way race, only 34% of the vote is needed, meaning that over 65% of the voters can be against a candidate, and they still would win. And as more candidates are in any particular race, this problem would only grow worse.

Thanks to FPTP, the level for victory is reduced. Therefore, it effectively encourages all sorts of dirty tricks, because the risk vs reward is so lop sided.

For example, with gerrymandering, a party can maintain control by creating safe districts that they do not have to worry about party opposition from. However, in so doing they put themselves at risk for primary challenges, with fringe candidates able to unseat party incumbents. This in turn forces ever more extreme positions by even moderate candidates, as they try and defend themselves from the fanatical wing. As a result, over time gerrymandering puts the entire party at risk as ever more extreme candidates take power, and produces officials which do not reflect the People they were elected to represent.

FPTP in effect forces a two-party dominance. This dominance is most clearly visible with the use of primary elections to control the political focus of a campaign. The political parties create the forums by which candidates can reach out to voters. They control the elections for which candidate will run on a particular parties ticket in the general election. To appear in the general election, one must win a primary which is controlled by political parties that may or may not reflect the values of the People. Primaries remain one of the least democratic systems we maintain, yet every election they become more and more prominent. The result is that party primaries have become a form of top-two run-off election, which in turn make closed, and controlled primaries ever harder to maintain as forces which would otherwise be external to the parties must join in, or else not have a voice come the general election.

Another issue which arises from FPTP is that wealth finds it very easy to buy influence. The super-rich have only two choices upon which to put their money on, after all. A large number hedge their bets, and donate to both parties to one extent or another. And this has been going on for a very long time. And then they use this influence to then keep FPTP, and the two-party dominance, in place. We find news articles from William Hearst's editorial board going back a century arguing against alternatives to FPTP, while today the dark money of Sheldon Adelson buys campaign ads to fight against campaign finance reform.

Ultimately, the wealthy use their monetary resources for furthering their own, greedy ends. And this does not even need to be so subtle as a newspaper editorial or magazine interview. They can simply use their wealth to overwhelm the opposition, shutting down the communication channels used by the opposition. It is not difficult for someone with even moderate wealth to swamp the public commons with their message.

As money breeds success in politics, so too does success encourage ever larger campaigns, with the pricetag continuing to soar. With soaring pricetags for political campaigns, this then makes politicians ever more dependent on these wealthy donors as well. It becomes a self-sustaining system, one which can not stand.

These factors together create a perfect storm by which our elected officials do not reflect the needs of those represented. They become beholden to political bosses, and large donors. After all, without their custom made voting districts, their primary support, and the money on their side, it would have been an uphill battle for the candidate as they can see it. There is no incentive to reach out to the voter, or to even care what the voter wants. The powers-that-be have made the election such a foregone conclusion that we witness an ever widening gulf between the People and office holder.

All due to the FPTP voting system.

This in turn disengages the People from the political process. Why vote, or care, when their voice is ignored? As the People become politically adrift, they begin following whims, become focused on a single issue, focus on the party labels, or even drop out from the process entirely. Without changing this apathy, no change can take root, and the People will forever be ignored.

With FPTP making elections safe for politicians, there is no incentive for them to be able to do their jobs. Which candidates pander to the party elites, and the monetary backers of campaigns go to the top of the pile. No candidate likes fundraising, or collecting endorsements, so they pick the easiest path forward. With large party blocks and wealthy donors enabling them to gain what is needed with less work, they come to dominante the process. This leads us to candidates which look good on a campaign poster and can give a speech, but have to rely upon others for doing even the basic parts of their job. Where else would these lackluster politicians turn to for help but the party and donors they already have worked with before? As a result neither of these two groups have any incentive for candidates with actual skill, intelligence, or even capable of independent thought.

To fix this, we have to change the very idea of what voting is.

The Constitution gives the qualification system for electors to be identical between the largest legislative branch and the federal officers. This means that any options for reform can be developed relatively simply on the state level, which in turn would reflect on the federal. And there is nothing in the Constitution requiring us to use the same system in every state. It would be smarter for us to diversify the solutions, allowing each state to develop a method that works best for the people they serve. And by diversifying, states can learn from each other, and that is something we all can appreciate.

To replace FPTP, we have several options to explore. Each option has both advantages, and disadvantages. With any system, the final form should be a compromise, taking the best elements of each, including from FPTP, which the people themselves wish to use.

By doing so, we can best study, and understand, what works for the People.

OPTION A: Proportional Voting

One of the first options to look at is proportional voting systems. In effect, instead of voting for a single seat, a person votes for a block of seats, and the breakdown by percentage gives us the final results. This sounds good on principle, but the devil is, as ever, in the details.

There are several options for proportional voting, but what we need to avoid are those which make political parties themselves part of the establishment. Using a political party approach to proportional voting, once entrenched, history shows that it becomes difficult to remove a party in power.

There is a proportional voting system which has historically shown itself not only solid, but doing so while avoiding the problem of political party entrenchment. And, it is as American as apple pie to boot. This system is called Single Transferable Voting (STV).

Starting in the 1920's, STV voting began growing in popularity, with 22 major cities across the United States adopting it at its peak, including the largest, New York City. A widespread campaign, lead by media giants such as the Hearst group, spent decades trying to stamp it out. Today, only two cities, Cambridge, Massachusetts and Minneapolis, Minnesota, retain STV. But, history has shown that for its goals, STV is proven in its results.

The way in which STV works is by having every voter with a single vote, but with election districts holding multiple seats, rather than the one-district, one-state approach we have today. Then, this vote can be transferred from a losing candidate to a subsequent choice. As a result, it is far more probable for a voter to have representation which reflects their viewpoint. As a result, STV is mathematically more likely to result in a more representative electoral result.

The trade off is that we will need to use math to decide STV election results. This math is open, however, so anybody can do it. But it does mean that the simple horse race approach to elections would no longer exist.

Let us make some district rules here. The more seats in a district, the more candidates would be running, and we do not want to see the results of 40 candidates in a single race to our sanity, so we set a rule by which a district should have no more than 7 seats. In order to minimize gerrymandering, we should aim for a minimum seat count at least 4 for when any body, be it a county or state, requires multiple districts. Then to prevent stacking the legislative body, all districts are required to be within 1 representative of each other. Additional districts cannot then be added until all current districts have 7 seats. Bodies with fewer than 7 officers to elect would therefore have a single district. Bodies with 8-14 seats would have two, 15-21 have three, etc.

Using this method, our largest state by population, California, would have 8 districts, 5 with 7 representatives and 3 with 6. Runner up Texas would have 6 districts in total. Florida and New York wind up with 4 districts each. Illinois and Pennsylvania would contain 3 districts each. We would find Missouri, Wisconsin, Tennessee, Maryland, Massachusetts, Minnesota, Arizona, Georgia, Mississippi, New Jersey, Indiana, Ohio, North Carolina, Virginia and Washington each with 2 districts. The remaining states would have only have a single at-large district through this manner. All without any change in how many representatives each state sends to Washington D.C.

For elections, these districts would be split up, percentage-wise, for setting the election threshold for winning one of these elected offices. So a district with 3 seats, you would need 33% of the votes to win, with 4 seat you would need 25%, 5 seats you would need 20%, and so forth. If a candidate meets this minimum threshold, that candidate wins the office. Once the initial allotment winners is determined, then votes begin being transferred. This sounds more complex than it sounds, so let us go with an example.

First, overvotes for a candidate are moved, proportionally. Let us use a district with 4 seats, wherein each candidate needs 25% to win a seat. We have 9 candidates for these 4 offices, and the breakdown is as follows (going from most votes to least, and using whole numbers and simple splits to simplify the example):

1	2	3	4	5	6	7	8	9
28%	21%	18%	10%	8%	6%	4%	3%	2%

As we can see, only Candidate 1 won outright, so we take his surplus of 3% and allocate it according to percentage to the secondary choices, with roughly 2/3rds of his voters supporting Candidate 8 and 1/3rd supporting Candidate 5, who get 2 and 1 percent respectively, resulting in this:

1	2	3	4	5	6	7	8	9
25%	21%	18%	10%	9%	6%	4%	5%	2%

With that concluded, we look at the lowest percentage candidate, Candidate 9, and drop him from the count. Those votes go to the majority secondary choice of Candidate 8, whom Candidate 9's voters found a solid moderate voice, giving us this result:

1	2	3	4	5	6	7	8	9
25%	21%	18%	10%	9%	6%	4%	7%	-

Now Candidate 7 has the lowest percentage. 7 was a single issue candidate, with his supporters otherwise also supporting Candidates 2 and 3 in roughly even numbers, resulting in each gaining 2 points, resulting in this:

1	2	3	4	5	6	7	8	9
25%	23%	20%	10%	9%	6%	4%	7%	-

Now Candidate 6 is the lowest. Most of 6's voters secondary choice was 1, but 1 has already won, so now we go to their third choice, and we find most of 6's voters supported Candidate 8, who now gains 5 points and the remainder mostly supporting Candidate 5, who gains 1 point. As we have now processed roughly half of the candidates, let us now review the current breakdown:

1	2	3	4	5	6	7	8	9
25%	23%	20%	10%	10%	-	-	12%	-

It is at this point we hit the first real problem. Candidate 4 was a fringe candidate with a rabid base of support who would not accept any other candidates. The candidate's positions were widely unpopular among the larger population. As such, those voters by and large did not put anyone in for a transferable vote - it was 4 or nobody for a sizable portion of this voting block. This also meant that few if any other candidates voters included 4 in their alternate choice either. In this case, their votes would work in much the same way as a first past the post system, they would be moved past in the count, and the tally percentages adjusted accordingly. This causes the other candidates to gain proportion, raising their totals:

1	2	3	4	5	6	7	8	9
28%	25%	22%	-	11%	-	-	14%	-

Candidate 2 has now won the second seat, with the exact number needed. However, now candidate 1 is once again over the limit. We need to now re-run his voters secondary choices in proportion, meaning that 2% goes to 8, and 1% to 5:

1	2	3	4	5	6	7	8	9
25%	25%	22%	-	12%	-	-	16%	-

This leaves Candidate 5 as the lowest. We again drop him, and allocate his votes to the candidate remaining which his voters supported, number 8:

1	2	3	4	5	6	7	8	9
25%	25%	22%	-	-	-	-	28%	-

Now 8 is over-limit, but we have 4 candidates left, the number of seats we needed to fill. At this point the math ends, and we have an election district with Candidates 1,2,3 and 8 as its representatives.

Going over this, we will note that in the initial count, Candidate 8 was the second lowest initially, but won a seat none the less. That is because 8 was a secondary or tertiary choice for many voters. As a result, we now have a district which now reflects the will of the voters, rather than one which is the result of political strategy to keep a candidate out of office, as we find in FPTP.

STV works well for legislatures, both the per-population based House of Representatives as well as the Senate. While the Senate has only two seats, the territory of Senators is not under question, nor can it be altered in any manner. As such, a proportional election method, with both Senate seats elected at the same time, but voters only casting a single vote for the election, would result in the US Senate better reflecting the voters of the states themselves.

The STV method better reflects voter desire than the traditional first-past-the-post methodology used in districts today, while minimizing the power of political parties to rig the system without eliminating their role. This would in turn enable more accurate representation of the people. And by being more representative, it engages the voter. Having a representative the voter understands and feels speaks for them means that voter will be engaged.

The use of STV also limits the impact of gerrymandering – as the large number of candidates involved makes not only it far more difficult to make partisan districts, if not near impossible. If anything, gerrymandering now becomes something more trouble than it is worth by making the drawbacks far more severe than the benefits.

The influence of money on the system becomes weaker as well under STV. By eliminating both the primary as well as adding multiple seats per district, any focus by monied interests becomes diluted. More channels they need to address means more difficult for any particular dollar to influence the outcome. Negative campaigns, the lions share of money raised going to, then also become far more problematic to implement, as now there is no horse race with a single winner.

With the elimination of the costly primary stage while also making the traditional money-backed campaigning no longer as effective, the drawbacks to not using this approach now clearly outweigh the benefits of maintaining the system as/is.

Obviously the states will set up their qualifications for their particular needs, as specified in the Constitution itself.

Recall this requires no amending of the Constitution whatsoever, and is only an interpretation of the document using modern eyes. And what it does, changes a lot more as we will see.

The issue with STV or any other direct election method is one of information overload. A voter is ultimately only as useful for the system as their understanding of larger concerns. Any elected official cannot do a single task, they must handle a variety of challenges. Yet, many elections for higher office boil down to very few issues for any single voter.

How can any single voter hope to understand the issues demanded on every single elected office level, and choose accordingly? The information needed would turn voting into a full time affair, between federal, state, county and local election issues.

Even with a more proportional system such as STV, we could find control falling into the hands of unelected elites, those who manage elections for all tiers of office. They would be the gatekeepers, even in a multi-party proportional system, and as a result can limit access to the information needed or steer the information to suit some single campaign issue.

Elections matter, yet we give less thought into our elected officials than we do into ordering our coffee in the morning. Every one of us picks some issue or a handful of issues, grabs onto it, and focuses on that. Most often, this comes with the same level of selection as ones favorite sports team. We root for "our team" and boo "the other team." And that's to be expected, due to the sheer volume of information needed for electing officials.

An STV election, even as proportionally representative as it would be in theory, would further aggravate this issue. Now with more candidates on the ballot, there would be far more information needed to sort through in order to make an educated choice. And we would need a far more engaged population than has been found in history. Let us then look at the other options.

OPTION B: Cellular Democracy

When we look at nations with the largest voter turnout, we do not find nations with direct elections for higher office. Instead we find the majority hold direct elections for local office, and indirect elections for higher. The political economist Fred Foldvary coined a term for such a system, labeling it a "Cellular Democracy" in his 1997 paper "Democracy Needs Reforming." The principle is that by focusing direct elections to the local level, it then becomes far easier to engage people directly, which in turn improves turnout. While common in nations such as China and Cuba such indirect elections are not alien to the United States, and are in fact used on the national stage even today.

Our nation's own founders rooted the Constitution on the work of philosophers such as John Stuart Mill, who advocated just such a system in his book "*Considerations on Representative Government*." We witness just this system in our Constitution's original method of selecting a Senator, where state legislatures pick those for office – an indirect selection. Voters would elect the members of one branch of government, which would then in turn elect the members of another, higher branch.

Such systems are used by several governments today. One such nation, Cuba, was listed as one of the best examples of a participatory democracy in the world just a few years ago. Another, China, manages the worlds largest population with few issues. The dynamic needs for two otherwise dissimilar nations do appear to be served well by cellular democracy.

How cellular democracies work is by leaving direct elections to the local level. These local officers would then elect higher offices. The city council elects your county, the county commissioners elect state legislators, and so on up to the top of the chain. We find this system already in effect for the selection of judges for the Supreme Court, with a caveat in place which we will come to in a moment.

When an indirect system is in place, one of two things can happen. Either party politics reigns supreme, or it dissolves to the point it no longer is a practical part of the body politic. Witness in Cuba, where there are multiple political parties, but election laws render all of them impotent in controlling the elections themselves. No party in Cuba can endorse or support a candidate for office, making Cuban political parties work more like caucuses within the United States. On the flip side we find China, where there is one political party, which operates as both an oversight committee and gatekeeper over the elections. Neither solution would be desired within the United States, so the lessons from them need to be learned.

Cellular Democracy directly addresses one of the fundamental issues of direct elections of higher offices, that the voters can and will make decisions based on individual demands, not collective. The higher the level of office, the more that the office being voted upon must look out for collective needs. Under our current system of

Democracy, many times those who hold higher offices pursue policy targeted at the level of the voter, that of the individual, rather than on the collective body politic.

We witness this in laws regulations which are designed not around a broad policy, but minute detail. Rather than, for example, a policy around different classifications of drug abuse, we witness laws focusing on specific forms of drugs such as crack cocaine being treated differently than powder cocaine, despite being exactly the same thing. A broader system should address drug abuse, not specific drugs.

By electing higher offices based on individualist needs, we get individualist elected officials, unable to work on broad principle. Politicians whose viewpoint is based around the individual, rather than the collective, will have difficulty understanding the need for broad spectrum solutions. Over time, this results in laws and policies which become unwieldy, addressing minor detail after minor detail, band aid fixes rather than addressing the root cause of an issue.

An indirect system however reduces this issue by limiting the range by which voters need to directly focus to the local level, one step above the individual or family unit we all work within every day. All politics is local politics becomes quite literal in Cellular Democracy.

As it is right now, an individual person is lost in the system among the throngs of electors. Their voice joins the cacophony, and gets drowned out by the noise. When your vote is one of millions, your voice is muted. But when your vote is now one of thousands for a council person, suddenly that elector now holds significantly more sway in elections. Through limiting the electors at each level, we have a system by which an individual elector matters far more. Then that council person matters to the County official who elected them. Once you continue up the chain, suddenly the individual voter has far more influence, as the collective is broken down into smaller groups which can form a consensus.

The reason why this works is due to our good friend mathematics once again.

Let us take a very simplistic model for a moment. We conceptualize a county made up of 4 towns and 1 city. Each of the towns have a population of 10,000, while the city has a population of 50,000. Each of these has a city council of 5 people, and the county has 5 seats. Each vote from these seats would be weighed by the population, so a town officer would have the weight of 2,000 people, while each city officer would have the weight of 10,000.

Under FPTP, the city would easily control all 5 seats, due to the overwhelming population. As a result, a minority viewpoint can step in, and lobby hard in a small area to gain full control. We witness this with the rise of fringe groups such as the Tea Party, NRA, ALEC and the Christian Coalition. They they in turn appear far more powerful and expansive than they really are.

In a proportional system, the city would have 2/3rds, either 3 or 4 of the seats, and would still dominate. While it would in part prevent the minority viewpoint takeover, it would not give the peripheral areas significant voice, and those voters would still be effectively marginalized.

Under a compartmentalized system, however, there is a higher probability for both of these smaller voices to be heard. If a minority voice had 60% support in three of the small towns, while only 20% of the county population, they could have a direct voice to several of the voting block. As well, it becomes far more easier for a peripheral area to get their message across. This would give such minorities a voice, but not at the expense of the majority.

In aggregate, the mathematics from Cellular Democracy would make it far more likely for higher level officers to address the needs by minority groups. And it does this without taking any individuals power away. In theory, this would make compromise far easier to accomplish, and prevents domination by any single group or organization over the long term.

What such a system might give us is a stable system better able to reflect the will of the people. Support will need to be popularized across the nation, rather than a minority of ideas or talents controlling the body politic. Minority interests will he easier to address without the need for them to dominate, and can no longer be easily marginalized. This in turn results in a highly stable system over the long term, one able to take the long view and address the issues which affect us all.

Some have said that our founders feared democracy, in giving full power to the mob directly. Studying their words, it can be said that some did feel this way. But in general, that was not the fear. Instead, their fear was in the ability of the masses to understand larger issues which undoubtedly would come along. Hence they set up a framework which would allow for those with the experience to handle longer term solutions. This form of merit-based appointment as envisioned by John Stewart Mill fell out of fashion as party politics began to dominate our nation. The result is our current system which fails to consider the merit of any particular candidate, and instead rewards popularity.

When the pool of people which these officers are held directly accountable to is smaller, there is less of a drive for pandering to the base. Lower officers operate as a form of firewall. The main concern however is that such a close relationship will breed familiarity, which is both a good and a bad thing. Familiarity is good when it imparts a level of trust that enables our government to get things done. Familiarity is bad when we find a "boys club" form, where people are kept in power not for their skill in legislating, but due to who they know. This is precisely why the 17th Amendment, making Senators directly elected, was passed.

Within the Constitution however, we get a clue for a solution to the negative aspects.

When the President nominates candidates for executive officers, ambassadors, or judges, including those who will sit on the Supreme Court, those candidates are vetted by the US Senate. This results many times in extreme candidates being blocked while more moderate ones then entering office. It is not perfect, but it has prevented more such candidates from taking office than let poor candidates in. So, let us consider if we apply this policy more broadly.

Candidates nominated would need to be vetted by lower officers. So, a county level officer would need to be vetted by the general voters of the city which nominated them directly, a state level would need to be vetted by city councils within the county which nominated, and so forth. This is, if you remember, the nomination period. After the nominees are vetted, then the election would be held. Every elector within these pools should be free to nominate someone to the election, but as with the Constitution, any particular entity would be prohibited from voting for candidates they nominate.

And for simple appointments, it would be even simpler. The appointment of, say, a state comptroller by its legislature would then be run past all county officials to approve or reject the appointment.

Then the main issue comes over endurance of office. We find this within the Supreme Court now, where a justice reveals themselves to have not adhered to the positions which put them into office in the first place. In some states, there are methods for recalling such politicians, but they are often times cumbersome and inflexible. There are other options however.

One of the simplest option available for handling an official which was not operating in good faith is to veto, or vote down that official. Ideally, this should be as broadly handled as possible, or on a set schedule. So, once a year or once every other year, voters have the option to, as a collective, veto an officer. This would be a collective vote of no confidence. This would not be an election for a new officer, or nomination, just a simple vote to remove a troublesome politician. This approach prevents the abuse we find in recall elections, while also enables the people to prevent the establishment of an unaccountable bureaucracy, out of touch with the people it is there to serve.

We do need something in place to prevent the handing control to the mob either. Public opinions swing after all, often times in a reactionary manner. Allowing for the people to petition for removal of a particularly troublesome elected official, a massive vote of no-confidence, does need to be listened to regardless. To prevent a whim of the electorate from removing an officer, such a vote needs to be of higher standard than simple majority. Using the Constitution as a guide, we should use the requirements of an impeachment proceedings. This means that such a vote would need a 2/3rd majority of the total voting population, not just of registered voters, to remove someone from office.

Even if the official survived such a recall, but gained a sizable opposition, it would be a warning that they are on the wrong track. If they do not clean up, they may not survive the next election. Let us be honest here, a politician would need to have messed up on a scale unimaginable for such an event to happen. We do not have the Senate remove a President from office without a 2/3rd majority of the entire Senate, not just of those in attendance, after all. By giving such a direct election, we would give politicians an indication of their future, of how their policies are viewed, and give them a chance to address the issues.

There are multiple avenues for handling this. Traditionally, a special election is held, but those cost time and money. It is not inconceivable for a political opportunist to exploit the process and attack an opponent. As a result of this excess and the chilling factor on public discourse, it should not be utilized.

In the modern era, we have immediate access to a huge amount of data, as well as direct access to electronic systems. An open-ended recall system would allow for the public to file their dissatisfaction at any time. Add in an undo, for a momentary lapse based on a whim, and the system should be able to self regulate. As politicians would have the information, they would know at any time how many of the people are against their current policies. More than opinion polls, more than a random sampling, a full and direct reference of how the politician stands from moment to moment.

As each election level is derived from the one directly below, it should in theory reflect the people under them. By having proportional representation, an immediate veto vote, as well as a recall system in place, the main issues of Cellular Democracy are addressed in a clean, and logical manner.

Direct systems, even proportional ones such as STV, require a significant amount of effort and education on the part of the voter to be aware of the issues and candidates on any particular election. Cellular Democracies in theory enable for a less educated population to still be governed well, with those more skilled at the jobs to be appointed to those jobs, rather than whomever looks better on television. If given a proper oversight system, Cellular Democracy has the potential to address the issues of governance, while staying within the bounds of the Constitution.

However, it in effect makes the nation run on a form of auto-pilot. Cellular Democracy is ultimately a lazy system, one optimized for those either unable to grasp the issues, or those without time to deal with the issues. And any lazy system, even one with controls in place, is one in which corruption can grow without notice, quietly, until it is pervasive. The work needed to root out such corruption then becomes greater than if we had just used a direct electoral system to begin with.

OPTION C: Authoritarian Democracy

There is another option as well, one which removes the People as part of the system entirely. This form of government is one which became popular in the 1920's, and was found in nations such as Italy and Spain. While we commonly use the phrase fascism or totalitarianism to describe Authoritarian Democracy as found in these two examples, we can find variants of this system in numerous other, non-fascist, states such as Singapore and Kuwait.

At its core, the Authoritarian Democracy puts central power into the hands of a select group. While they do not directly rule, their ability to elect whom does rule gives them incredible levels of power and authority.

The Italian model is one of the most thoroughly examined and understood, so it is the one we will use here.

This authority was granted to an unelected body, called the "Grand Council of Fascism." Each member was appointed to a 3-year term, and were members of the government, political party leaders, and the heads of large corporations through the Royal Academy of Italy. By doing so, these unelected members could then direct the nature of the nation.

As these various authorities were considered the elite of Italy, they were considered to have the foresight to help guide the nation. As they had earned significant wealth through their corporate interests, the idea was that they were superior in some fashion to other people, and therefore should rule.

These experts would then elect the civil government. By not being the government themselves, it would not, so goes the theory, descend into an absolute dictatorship. The belief was such that this would give the benefits of an elected government without the mob rule that it was claimed would be found in typical democracies.

In practice however, the quality of the government depended greatly on who these elites are. Using classic Eugenic thought, as Nazi Germany did, their leadership council believed that some form of pseudoscientific purity was the standard by which the authority should be selected. Using wealth as the metric, Italy put its wealthiest people in charge. Spain utilized a head of household concept, with clan heads and corporate leaders given positions within their National Council.

An example of modern day Authoritarian Democracy can be found in Singapore. Cabinet of Singapore members are appointed by the Prime Minister or President directly. The Cabinet is filled with corporate executives from a myriad of fields, from medical to engineering.

Singapore differs from Italy in that while the Cabinet appoints the bureaucracy and ministries of government, there remains a check on them in the parliament, which is directly elected by the population at large. It is a weak check however, with this Cabinet authorizing which political parties can run for office. But the check remains in place, theoretically, should a situation ever arise under which Singapore's Cabinet should overstep its authority, or even worse engage in behavior which outrages the population.

By controlling the ministries, the Cabinet wields incredible levels of power. But with its appointment being from one of two people, it does not well reflect the people of Singapore. With the parliament little more than a last resort block, it does not meet the goal we have set for ourselves here.

Now, we could look at Authoritarian Democracy and decry it as being so radically different from how our republic has run that it could not possibly be constitutional. However, it actually could be Constitutional. Recall, the standards for who is an elector is set by the states themselves, with the same standards put forth for federal office as that states own government. A state which incorporated an "Oversight Committee" into its election process would, in fact, be free to implement an Authoritarian Democracy. And, with the formation of specialized committees and counsels which create legislation, wrangle elections, and force obedience by our elected officials, one realizes that this is precisely the system which we find the Oligarchs steering us in the direction of.

Look at the situation under Governor Snyder in Michigan. Thanks to Michigan Public Act 436 of 2012, he can appoint unelected officials to manage various elected responsibilities. Despite his program being overturned by voters, he utilized parliamentary tricks to retain it, while eliminating the voters ability to overturn his decisions. And who developed this idea but the American Legislative Exchange Counsel, precisely the kind of organization which is the backbone of Authoritarian Democracy. Now that he could overturn elected officials, it is not hard to imagine this authority expanding, with elections not having any power across the state.

There are some elements which could be utilized, but the system here, despite being fully workable under the US Constitution, rejects what our founders stood for.

A new monarchy of the wealthy, an Oligarchy of by and for the rich. All easily done, if we do not take care.

ISSUES BEFORE US

Beyond knowing what options there are, we need to know the issues that are at hand. These problems are persistent, and have been with us sometimes since the beginning of our nation. Over time, these problems have led us to a political process we find today, where people often times feel isolated from the system that only works when they participate.

ISSUE: Redistricting

One of the core problems in any system is in how you district people for voting.

The first problem is that there is no unified system for setting up election districts. Each state is free, under the Constitution, to develop their own approach to redistricting. One option long established was to piggyback district allotment on top of existing municipalities, counties, and unincorporated areas. Unfortunately, a law passed in 1967 (2 U.S. Code § 2c) called the "Uniform Congressional District Act" now prohibits multi-member districts, despite being historically normal throughout US history. This makes piggybacking districts on top of existing lines far more of a challenge, if not impossible.

By congress passing the UCDA, they have severely hamstrung the ability of the states to develop their own systems. Also, arguably, the law has made several states elections of federal officers unconstitutional, due to those elections no longer being based on the same system as used to elect their own legislators. Washington State is one such state, which uses two legislators per district.

This measure was passed out of fear that states would create at-large districts designed to marginalize minority voting populations. However, the way in which it was done has introduced new problems, and is hurting our system overall.

A change to the UCDA could address this issue, while also preserving the goals set forth in the passing of the Act in the first place. Here is the act as/is:

> *In each State entitled in the Ninety-first Congress or in any subsequent Congress thereafter to more than one Representative under an apportionment made pursuant to the provisions of section 2a(a) of this title, there shall be established by law a number of districts equal to the number of Representatives to which such State is so entitled, and Representatives shall be elected only from districts so established, no district to elect more than one Representative (except that a State which is entitled to more than one Representative and which has in all previous elections elected its Representatives at Large may elect its Representatives at Large to the Ninety-first Congress).*

Now, with some slight adjustments, my suggestion is to adjust the text to this:

> *In each State entitled in the One-hundred Fifteenth Congress or in any subsequent Congress thereafter under an apportionment made pursuant to the provisions of section 2a(a) of this title, there shall be established by law that each elector for Representative may only have cast a single vote for Representative, nor elect more than one Representative.*

This simpler approach reintroduces flexibility in our districts, while preventing the issue raised in 1967 of a state selecting to be purely at-large, and then enabling a majority population to completely marginalize a minority from representation. Now states would be free to experiment with multiple options, and then would be better positioned to create election districts that better reflect the underlying borders. In addition, by tying state legislative and US congressional districts to these lower districts, rather than remaining independent of them, it would help prevent redistricting dilemmas which currently cause political conflicts within our nation.

These lower districts continue to a level of discrete precincts, very tiny voting areas which hold a small group of people ranging from a few hundred to a few thousand people. These precincts are the closest level to the people, set up by a small geographic area. And by doing so, this makes redistricting much simpler for the state to manage. The boundaries of any given district are less likely to change from one census to the next due to this smaller area of coverage.

So, we have precincts which do not shift often, all contained within cities, counties and states which do not shift at all. So, let us attach districts in a vertical manner from this. So, a city has precincts within it, a county has cities within it, and states have counties within them. Districts would need to be formed by grouping these together, in a vertical manner. So, a state's congressional district would have several legislative districts contained therein. A legislative district would have several county districts contained within. And the county's districts would have several city districts, and precincts, contained within. The borders must, to be fully compliant with the Constitution, be tied to each other. So, a legislative district can be within a congressional district, but it cannot go out of that same congressional district and gain territory found within another. A county district is within a Legislative, but it cannot reach over into another one. Down the line it goes.

By tying districts to each other, top to bottom, gerrymandering attempts would affect state, county and even local officials on a broad level. Manipulation of the congressional delegation becomes far more problematic when a state representative is putting their own district on the line in the process. This then comes back to risk vs reward. As it becomes far harder to develop these specialized, rigged districts, with reduced payout due to systems like STV, fewer will attempt to engage in gerrymandering. And without the benefit of a narrow group of candidates, without the primaries to downselect candidates, and without safe districts, moneyed interests would now find the cost for "business as usual" climbing into the stratosphere.

Combining this approach with one of a myriad approaches to proportional elections, such as STV, the people would have representation which is statistically more likely to reflect their own views. A very good thing for all involved.

ISSUE: Oversight

All of the options presented, plus our existing system, have merits in their favor. If we study them, we can pull together a theoretical design of government which could give us a stronger republic, one which better reflects the People.

Each idea has something which is of use to us. When we look at nations which use proportional democracy, we find the size of the voting pool itself becomes a hindrance. When we look at nations which use indirect democracy, we find a system which limits the reflection of the People. When we look at authoritarian democracy, we see an elite in charge. All of them have flaws. And yet, all of them offer a piece to the puzzle.

What we face however is the problem of how do you maintain such a system? It might be that taking a page out of the authoritarian democratic book is the right answer. The reason why authoritarian democratic systems are stable is due to the unelected body being involved in some oversight and planning capability. Free from the concern over the voter, they can take a longer term view of a situation. We do not want appointment over officials, for that brings abuse and corruption. But in a narrow role such a body might work.

At this time, oversight over our nations electoral process is handled by political appointments or political parties themselves. Similarly, long term planning is also handled by these same groups. As a result, both processes are easy to abuse, with those in power given incentive to leverage these processes for their own gain.

There are a few areas where this does not happen however, the most notable of which is the Federal Reserve. For the reserve, instead we have appointments to the various chairs, appointments which extend beyond any political office term. And these appointments are on a rotating basis, so no single legislature or President will be able to appoint more than a fraction of the total. Admittedly, the Reserve has its own issues tied to the banking industry itself, but for the purposes of appointments, it is a suitable model to follow.

This is precisely the kind of body needed to oversee our electoral process, vetting candidates, and keeping an eye on the system itself. On paper, we have such a body, the Federal Election Commission. But in practice, it is partisan, and deadlocked. The existing design is built upon political party membership, and as such it becomes increasingly easy for issues to arise that neuters its effectiveness. Add in that the punitive measures often times cannot be taken until after an election is over, a reactionary system, and are incredibly narrow in options to boot, the FEC fails to fulfill its statutory duty.

To help the FEC, the government did found the Election Assistance Commission in 2002. However, as an independent body from the FEC, rather than part of the existing agency, we find that this new body is similarly unable to make headway against the problems before it. The system continues to be plagued with issues that are only growing worse over time. We need a far stronger body. It should be modeled on a merged FEC and EAC, but with both a greatly expanded membership and the power to preempt offenses.

The members of this body would be considered federal officers, operating as a Judicial office under the direct supervision of the Supreme Court, a similar arrangement as the Electoral Court in Brazil, Electoral Institute in Mexico and the Constitutional Council in France. By virtue of being a federal office, membership in such a body would prohibit a serving legislator, supreme court justice, or member of the executive branch, from serving on the body. As a Judicial Office with members appointed by the Court itself, it would have the power and authority to enforce decisions, and could now proactively prevent issues beforehand.

This role needs to be a full time focus for members. The office holders must be prohibited from running for office both while serving on this body and for at least one full election cycle after serving. Further, members of this body must be prohibited from working in the private sector, again, both while serving for this agency as well as for at least one full election cycle after serving.

While the idea of appointment by the president sounds good in theory, in practice this is automatically going to create a partisan slant to any body so appointed. France here gives us the most ready avenue to avoid this, where members of this body are themselves former elected officials, including previous Presidents. Tying participation in this with access to a former elected federal officials pension would make a ready body of agents willing to be members of this body.

It would not just be a singular council, but would have lower agencies that would operate on the state level. By being made up of people who had been elected in the past, they would be intimate with both the mannerisms and mechanisms of abuse. By tying their pension to membership on this council, it would reduce the revolving door from our halls of government to corporations which then use our former politicians as lobbying agents. Require a set term to sit upon the council, say three election cycles, 6 years, and one term off the council without running for office or working in the private sector, 2 more years, before their pension becomes permanent. Combine with the prohibition on re-entering office directly from the organization, and on working for a private body, for a full election cycle after serving, the issues of lobbying would be reduced.

The President should maintain the ability to appoint the chairman of this revised FEC, but only the chairman. Like the Federal Reserve, the FEC chairman should be appointed in the first month of the last year of a President's term, to then serve through the majority of the next. And as this is only a chairman, with the other positions decided by the greater body of former politicians from amongst themselves, the power of the President to influence the body is minimal.

The issue then is to make sure that it does not become a power unto itself. This is why the limitation on membership to former politicians, and ban upon attempts to run for office, or participation in the private sector. By tying a generous pension package to participation, with these restrictions in place, it becomes self-enforcing. To prevent rule changes, by it being a Judicial office with an executive appointed chairman, such rule changes will require the approval of all three branches of government.

It would then serve to create, and oversee, election policy. It is time we admit that our courts reliably are the arbiters of what elections are, what is allowed, and as such, through this agency they would then be more proactive in the proscribing of solutions. As it is now, courts cannot act until it is far too late. But without judicial action, the institutions of democracy slowly decay.

Enabling this body to be more active would allow the heading off of issues before they grow into problems. An ounce of prevention is worth a pound of cure, as the adage goes. The agency would need to vet candidates for ballots, oversee the ballot box, and even help handle precinct allocation.

Realize that with the push for more representative democracy, this organization would have a critical, but nearly transparent role in our democracy. Their proactive capability combined with the judicial powers wielded would serve well in preventing payola programs, bribes, and similar. Election bosses would become impotent, and it simply would not serve for parties to continue as they have.

Over time, the merging of these systems in this manner would result in the emergence of a more robust, and representative democracy in this country. And it would happen all in line with our Constitution as it is, without the need to amend.

ISSUE: Case Law

This book presents an original interpretation for the US Constitution, based not on the history of case law, or of traditional methods, but by bringing a new outlook to bear upon it. But by itself, it is just a study without real strength. To bring any ideas presented here forward, one must understand how it is that interpretations are introduced, and that is through case law, also known as common law or legal precedent.

Case law, also known as Common Law, are court decisions which when added together make for a common interpretation of law. This can further be extended and, as set forth in the landmark case of *McCullough vs Maryland*, the Constitution itself is to be interpreted by the Supreme Court, an idea put forth by many of our founding fathers such as Alexander Hamilton and James Madison.

What this means is that when a court makes a decision, it looks to prior court decisions to build upon. However, this also means that the court can only make such a decision when ideas, interpretations are presented to it however. For example within *United States vs Miller*, the famous gun control debate case which overturned handgun restrictions. Both sides made the argument that the 2nd Amendment was over gun ownership. As a result, the court had to decide based on gun ownership, not if the amendment was on ownership at all. The late Justice Antonin Scalia himself noted this issue within the courts decision.

These case decisions add up over time, and the more decisions are built upon each other, the more entrenched an idea becomes. This means the more work is needed to overturn them. Patience is a virtue when dealing with such entrenched ideas. Many times good ideas, good interpretations, are abandoned not because they did not work, but because the people involved in it simply were not patient enough. Other times, bad ideas were introduced because those involved were patient, such as the disaster of prohibition. It is a knife which cuts both ways.

We have our current system due to case law and tradition, not due to what is written in either the US Constitution nor in US Code. The way to fix the system is often times not over who is right or wrong, but over who is willing to put the work in to establish their idea, or to overturn established ideas, through case law.

If the ideas here are to be adopted, in whole or part, the area in which we would need to focus is not on revolutionary acts, but on the simple acts found in the courtroom.

ISSUE: Electoral College

One of the least understood and least democratic areas of our government can be found in the electing of our President, the Electoral College. As found in Article 2, the Electoral College selects the president, with its members elected directly by the people as their proxy. The problem comes in that most states allocate by a winner-take-all, or WTA, model, that which candidate gets the most votes within a state gets all of the states electors. As a result, the focus comes down to a handful of swing states.

There is a movement to get rid of, or change the Electoral College to a direct, popular vote. Such a move is not only unwise, it would in the long term be an utter disaster.

Such a move to popular vote would effectively lock in a two-party system, giving incredible power to the two major political parties and rendering opposition effectively counter-productive. A three way race for President could either have one candidate winning with over 60% of the people voting against them. Or, if we carried forward the 50%+1 we have from the Electoral College, the race would be thrown to the house due to failing to meet the threshold of support. Then nobody's choice for President would be used.

Nations which use popular vote presidencies tend to decay into dictatorship in short order, if they do not collapse entirely. Look at the bloody history of Latin America, where widespread adoption of the Presidential system of government with direct elections. Of them, only a single one, Costa Rica, has avoided such a fate, and it did so by severely limiting the power of the Presidency. One of the reasons why the United States has endured has been the fact that we have the Electoral College, which prevents such minority control over our very strong Executive branch.

There is a perception that how the Electoral College works is set within the Constitution, or controlled by the Federal government. The people who push for an amendment to eliminate the Electoral College entirely hold this perception. What they fail to remember is that the Electoral College is controlled by rules set within each of the 50 states, for that state and that state alone. To change the system, the laws must be modified within each of our states under the Constitution. And not all of our states use the winner take all approach.

For example, in Nebraska and Maine the Presidential Electoral votes are allocated per congressional district, called Congressional District – Popular or CDP voting, so whomever gets the most votes in a district, no matter how few votes they actually get, gain that districts Elector. This sounds workable until consider the issue of gerrymandering. Should such a system become widespread, it would encourage gerrymandering, a problem we are trying to eliminate. And it would also continue to force a two party system due to the adherence of a First Past the Post methodology. All it does is to break down the size of the districts used, from state to congressional, without addressing the underlying problem.

But it is not the only solution. An alternative approach has been proposed several times, such as in Pennsylvania back in 2013, called "Proportional Popular – Popular," where Electors are allocated proportionally with the popular vote within the state itself. As a result, if you get 25% of the vote, you get 25% of the electors. And instead of it being a popular vote, with the minority control that multiple candidates would result in, we gain options to ensure that democracy is solidified rather than stifled.

While the forementioned STV system works well for an elected body with multiple seats, it simply would not work for the executive office. As the executive is elected as a single person, there will always be some level of representation disconnect. If the executive cabinet were elected piecemail, similar to how other nations elect an executive council or Presidium, this could be resolved in a more straightforward manner, but we are here to deal with the Constitution as/is, not how we wish it were.

Such a proportional election method without the winner-take-all state methodology we currently employ, is probably the only real solution we can offer without changing the very nature of our electoral system. Proportional voting would be a retrofit upon our existing system, and would in turn improve upon our system without requiring a major overhaul.

We need a majority of 50%+1 to win the office of both President, and Vice-President, but elections are not for the presidential candidate themselves, but on electors for these candidates – the electoral college. Indeed, with a proportional system the electoral college would serve a stronger role for our Republic. As each state has multiple electors, and they are elected in a block, the need for districting systems such as needed for STV is not there, so electors can be voted proportionally within each state directly.

Rather than a direct selection, or winner-take-all, we have the electors for a candidate allocated by voter preference. Each candidate will need to prepare their list of Electors for each Electoral College district ahead of time. Not the party, the Candidate themselves. We need to remove Party strength here. While yes, a party may have some influence, the candidates themselves need to hold final say over who will and will not be their Elector.

A candidate who is unable to provide a sufficient elector list to the states directly would therefore not be eligible for office within the Electoral College district. State laws would remain in place, so these electors would need to be citizens of that state, after all. For the candidates who lack people within a state to present as electors, there would simply be nobody for someone to cast their votes for. Candidates with no ground support, gimmick candidates who enter the presidential race but have no real support network, would be effectively eliminated from the system in a Constitutional manner.

This approach would however also open up the door for strong single issue candidates who wish to make their needs voiced. They could focus attention in an effort to make an impact on the national election, without risking the larger picture or requiring their voters from needing to consider strategic voting as found in the FPTP system. Never doubt the power of the lone Elector to bring an issue into the spotlight.

A proportional approach if adopted more widely would result in a far more democratic system than a simple popular vote solution. One potential problem with a popular-vote approach is that if we retain the current 50%+1 approach required within the Constitution for the Electoral College, and no candidate gets more than 50% of the vote, the House of Representatives gets to pick our president (look at the elections of 1992, 1996, and 2000, where no candidate had over 50% of the vote to get an idea of how this would look). Strong multi-party systems would make it impossible for any party to win the Presidency by vote, and Congress gets to pick instead.

Alternatively, if only whomever gets the majority of votes is the winner, regardless of percentage, it becomes WTA on a grand scale, where any third party candidate directly hurts their own voters. Three way races could be won with as little as 34% of the vote. 4 way, 26%, and so forth. This would force all politics into a two-party roadmap, and hurt electoral participation as people would rightly feel that they have little to no voice. We have witnessed the issues of a two party system within this nation already, with money and power brokered like trading cards between super-wealthy individuals. This cannot be sustainable, and the risk for collapse would eventually become too great.

Under a proportionally allocated Electoral College, even multi-party elections would be not only workable, but trivial to handle. Something long forgotten is that Electors can be repledged to another candidate. Simply put, electors for one candidate can be given to another with the permission of the candidate they were elected for. We have had this occur as far back as the election of Thomas Jefferson, where Jefferson and Aaron Burr split their electors, resulting in Jefferson as President, and Burr as Vice President.

This form of coalition presidency would give third parties a place in executive elections they lack now. A large elector candidate who lacked the 50%+1 would then need to negotiate with candidates who have fewer electors, and that means concessions, be it policies, legislature, cabinet posts, ambassadorships, judges, etc. It would also empower minor parties for their participation, which in turn would encourage voter engagement.

Let us use a real world election as an example. In the 1992 election, the winner, Bill Clinton, only won with 43% of the vote. Going on a state by state breakdown, Clinton would have gained, roughly, 229 electors. George HW Bush had 38.5% of the popular vote, and tabulating on a per-state level we find him with 198 electors. Neither would have had the 270 electors needed, due to the strong showing by H. Ross Perot, who under this approach would have gotten 101 electors. (America First candidate James Gritz would have gotten 1 elector from Utah and 9 electors are up in the air, with the margin too close for such a simple breakdown) To get the needed electors, the top two candidates would have needed the support of Ross Perot. For his electors, Perot could have forced concessions in either party, such as a number of cabinet positions or to scuttle NAFTA (a major part of his campaign).

This model clearly worked in the 1992 election, but how does it work in a far closer competition? To compare, let us use the 2000 election. Gore lost that election, despite winning the popular vote, due to several issues from a low turnout to voter purges in key states and quite possibly a spoiler effect from Ralph Nader's heavy turnout in Florida and New Hampshire. Under this model, we have Gore coming out with 259 electoral votes, Bush with 256, Nader holding 13, and 6 up in the air. Nader now becomes kingmaker, or not, because the only candidate he can give his electors to and put over the top is Al Gore. Combining the 256 of Bush with Nader's 13 would only get us to 269 electoral college votes, still not enough to win. So, Gore and Nader would be forced into an alliance, pulling the total to 272 electoral college votes, or else the election would be thrown to Congress. We cannot know the minds of these men, and what would have happened, but it is quite probable that such a bargaining could have resulted in scenarios such as Nader replacing Lieberman as Vice President, along with considerable concessions in platform, policy, and cabinet appointments.

Instead of a spoiler effect, this approach would give minority candidates a specific and important role in the system. The elimination of the spoiler effect would reinforce our democracy over time. Empowering minority parties would encourage voter participation through enabling these often times narrow and specialized parties.

There is another advantage to this system when it comes to voting fraud. Even if fraud and voter suppression does occur in any election, the total shift in a single state usually comes down to a few percentage points. That means in almost all states, voting problems will not change the result by enough to move even a single elector from one candidate to another, so would not affect the result of the election. In addition, those who would engage in fraud no longer could target 1 state to manipulate and get all of their electors. As a result, the most that voting fraud could accomplish in a single state is 1, maybe 2 electoral votes, and that only would be possible in very high population states with narrow margins. Proportional electors suddenly makes voting fraud too much work once you consider the potential reward balanced against the risk.

To show how, let us look at the 2004 election. There are claims that Bush won in 2004 due to voting fraud in Ohio, by manually editing the voting result during a data blackout, tipping the election through a few thousand votes spread across the entire state, handing Bush all of Ohio's 20 electoral votes. However, we must remember that Bush won the popular vote nationwide, with 62 million votes against Kerry's 59 million. The claimed total shift in Ohio was less than 100,000 votes. This means that if the claims of voting fraud are true, and Kerry was to win Ohio by a narrow margin, it would have been an inverse of 2000. Another candidate holding popular support would not have won the election due to WTA electors. But, using proportional electors, we have a result of Bush with 280 electoral college votes against Kerry's 257, with 2 up in the air. The popular candidate would have won, and should voting fraud be attempted, it becomes incredibly difficult to overturn the will of the people through deception and fraud.

Right now, most states are all but ignored in presidential elections, due to the predominance of WTA electoral college elections within most states. This means that elections focus on our population centers, large cities and metropolitan areas, and on the few states which have margins close enough to swing to either side in an election. This is not democratic, it is not empowering, and over the long term it can only hurt the voice of the people. Even the minority political voices in our nation deserve their say at the ballot box.

I believe in Democracy, and in the voice of the people. The proportional allocation approach to the Electoral College is simply the best solution for our nation.

FINAL THOUGHTS

Our nation is built on the words of men for the hopes of the people. Built on the ideals of the Enlightenment, our Constitution remains relevant today. What is missing however is the critical eye, to imagine another way for this faded document to be read. Without this eye, which dares to view our framework in a new way, there is no doubt that one day there will rise a Constitutional crisis that we cannot recover from.

Once our nation accepts the arguments of the Oligarchs without question, the experiment of a nation directed by the masses and not the classes shall come to an end. We must question, must study, and most of all must imagine a new day. The words of our Constitution were not written on stone, immutable, but in the blood found in each of our veins.

Native or immigrant, rich or poor, the Constitution is written for each of us. Nowhere in there can we find for the wealthy to have power over the poor, and it is high time we reminded people of that.

We The People are who are in charge, not those with the large bank accounts nor those born into nobility – a dictatorship of the proletariat as envisioned by Lieutenant Colonel Joseph Weydemeyer, a prominent member of the early Republican Party. It is high time we reminded the Oligarchy whose blood our Constitution, the People's Constitution, is written in.

www.ingramcontent.com/pod-product-compliance
Lightning Source LLC
Chambersburg PA
CBHW060312290526
45789CB00001B/496